This little book is dedicated to all those working safely and sanely for a safe and sane world.

THE DAY THE WORLD WENT SANE

by

Harry Barba

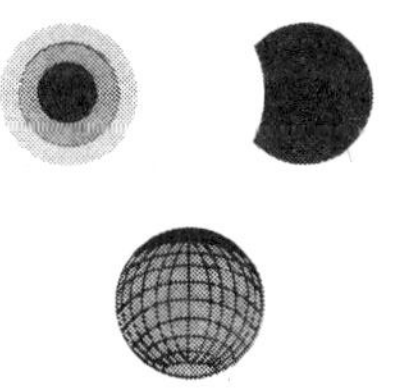

HARIAN CREATIVE PRESS
("One World Is Better Than None")
Adirondack-Metroland, Saratoga Springs, N.Y.,1979

Mailing Address:
47 Hyde Blvd.
Ballston Spa, N.Y. 12020

First Printing, Jan 1, 1979
Printed in the United States of America

ISBN 0-911906-14-2, Casebound
ISBN 0-911906-13-4
LIBRARY OF CONGRESS NUMBER LC 78-70762

Other Books by Harry Barba

- FOR THE GRAPE SEASON
- THE BULBULS
- 3 BY HARRY BARBA
- LOVE, IN THE PERSIAN WAY
- HOW TO TEACH WRITING IN THE TIME IT TAKES--
- TEACHING IN YOUR OWN WRITE
- THE CASE FOR SOCIALLY FUNCTIONAL WRITING, EDUCATION AND CULTURE
- TWO CONNECTICUT YANKEES TEACHING IN APPALACHIA
- ONE OF A KIND--THE MANY FACES AND VOICES OF AMERICA

FOREPIECE

Harry Barba wrote the first draft of ALLHALLOWSMAS in the summer of 1953. This draft presented the dialogue and interaction between THE MAN and THE WOMAN of Stage I, II, and III of ALLHALLOWSMAS and was titled THAT TIME OF YEAR. In the spring of 1961, the Drama School of the University of Iowa put on a closed production of THAT TIME OF YEAR for an audience of five hundred graduate students, teachers of drama, and three visiting N.Y. drama critics. The author revised the play into its present version and re-titled the play ALL OF US (AND ALL OF THEM) TOGETHER in 1973. In 1977, he gave the play its final revisions. And so we have a dramatic opera now titled ALLHALLOWSMAS.

THE DAY THE WORLD WENT SANE is the major work in ths book of two. Yet the reader might best go to it after ALLHALLOWSMAS. The reason becomes obvious even in a casual reading — the two works are related thematically in that sequence. ALLHALLOWSMAS was written before and thematically leads up to THE DAY THE WORLD WENT SANE. Though the author revised ALLHALLOWSMAS several times over two decades, THE DAY THE WORLD WENT SANE came out of the typewriter word for word as it appears in this book. The writing required a concentrated sequence of six months of uninterrupted effort. You might say the fictive ballet wrote itself.

What else? The author confesses to having been moved deeply in writing the first drafts of each. Revisions were done with loving care. The publishers suggest the reader consult the author's preface to The Harian Press July 4, 1976 edition of the author's collected short fiction, ONE OF A KIND--THE MANY FACES AND VOICES OF AMERICA. ALLHALLOWSMAS is the play referred to in the preface. Like ALLHALLOWSMAS, THE DAY THE WORLD WENT SANE is an outgrowth of the credo of socially functional writing, to be known from now on as SOC FUNC LIT.

The Publishers
HARIAN CREATIVE PRESS
Jan.1, 1979

THE DAY
THE WORLD WENT SANE
(A fictive ballet)

THE DAY THE WORLD WENT SANE

During the six day rally across from the Cape, we hardly noticed the tide, coming and going with the moon. The waters fed our campfires with driftwood, our curiosities with shells. This was enough. As for the seagulls, remarkable any were left. Normalcy the exception, the birds were taken as harbingers of good.

Sunset of the six day— The seagulls vanished, the tide stood absolutely still. The sky empty, the waters lay like lead. Demonstrators thrust sticks wrapped with shirts and blouses into campfires and held them flaming against the sky.

And so the beginning of the chain of bad events. I was used to the Time Machine-resurrected Living Presences playing their little games of in-'n-out. Delicate and ethereal, they tended to overreact, this I could understand. But then they literally vanished into thin air—my impatience deepened to worry. They'd never before dropped out of sight during a crisis of magnitude, I should've been alerted. Since Lt. Bartleby Bratt was second in command aboard Titan X, I was personally as well as politically hung up. As a result, I did not miss the Living Presences until it seemed too late.

Besides, the rally seemed a great success.

We responded to each speaker with rhythmic clapping. Tidal calls sent seagulls bursting upwards on all sides. Winds buffeted them out to sea, only to return them moments later.

And so it went, sunrise to sunset.

Days we cooked meals over community campfires, nights we crawled into pup tents and family campers. Others sprawled on the sands. We fell asleep to the hissing and soughing of the waves. Mornings we awoke to more driftwood, still another deposit of underwater sea creatures. Building campfires, boiling coffee, we made necklaces, wrist, and ankle bands of the shells—and collages, of the strange creatures. Scattered among us, seagulls circled for breakfast leavings as we waited for the first of that day's speakers.

And so, into the second week.

The morning of the day before the scheduled launching, we awoke with a new sense—the seagulls had vanished. As one, we turned to face Titan X across the swollen tides.

I was dumb with awe. All week I'd been expecting the reappearance of the Living Presences. Now I was sure, an event so horrendous was impending they'd retreated all the way of spacelessness and timelessness.

I yearned for a sight of just one of them, never mind their antics to beguile the world's stark terror. Even young Marco Polo—reading from the latest edition of his life, spread in his palms like a psaltery—would've been welcome. And I missed—how I missed—young Isaac Newton, supermarket bag of apples tucked under his arm. And all the others, I hungered for them with my soul.

At noon still no signs of my protégés, my surdity seethed. I had resurrected them to help out in just such a crisis. The time for levity and games was over.

At sunset, when one of the young demonstrators strode up the dune and began to speak, I nearly soughed with the tide. The leader of the Youthniks-in-Peace-and-World-Sanity called for dumping all "sectarian grievances," Project Survival Humankind. New firebrands flamed like votive candles.

That night was long and fateful. The opaque tides rising and falling again, the seagulls began returning. Several speakers later, the gulls cluttered the sands and filled the heavens.

Still no sign of the Living Presences.

Just after midnight, the tide was still as eternity. The current spokeswoman for the feminist took her turn. Right after, the World War II novelist, turned actor, turned mayoralty candidate, turned movie producer, director and actor, now a Party-Of-One Presidential Candidate. By the time he sat down, the tide had turned and was roiling and soughing back to sea.

An hour before dawn, the much-married centarian Supreme Court justice steadied himself with a dove-like hand on the shoulder of his girl bride. Tautening in the silken cage of his life, he clarioned like an old but never-to-be-daunted nightingale.

He called for a special demonstration march to follow immediately after the launching. We would encircle the headquarters of the Premier of the United Powers of the West and the headquarters of the Chairman of the United Forces of the East. In this way to remind the two leaders of our continuing vigil to insure peace and sanity. We would not let them forget it took but two fingers to push the buttons launching technological warfare. One finger was in the West, the other in the East.

As the old man swayed to the rhythms of what might be his last public plea, Titan X disappeared and reappeared, back and forth. Towering a multiple times as tall as the Statue of Liberty, straight up into the sky from the shoreline, looming over the bay like a gargantuan bullet, the atomic space ship put us into its shadows. Yet when the old man swayed toward us, the grisly machine was blotted out.

To reappear but a moment later. Now you see it, now you don't. Now you don't, now you do.

At that moment, I had a sense— It took but a man, the right, man, to make even Titan X's portentousness vanish. For a machine was, after all, only a machine. No matter how complex and powerful the mechanism, no machine was the match of a feeling and thinking man saying the right things at the right time. And that made all the difference.

But the next moment, the thought again— Still there were those two poised fingers.

Through my revelation, a glimpse of the eternal presidential candidate of the American Party. Looking like a wounded but still crowing rooster, he maneuvered his motorized wheelchair up the dune. Scurrying down the other side, he scuttled amidst Asiatic and African delegates. The beach became turbulent with *saris* and *dashikis*, with suddenly flurrying and screaming seagulls.

The birds thrust upwards. Three left behind on the sands, two struggled with the third to help it to become airborne. A sudden wind rising, all three finally soared wheeling and screaming among their kind.

Turning away, I faced Titan X.

Suddenly across the finger of sand connecting the Cape with our shore, young Bartleby Bratt, head thrown back, mouth opening and closing.

As he ran to us, I felt a deep chill. My mouth opened and closed in dumb echo of his. He was heading straight for me.

I'd started the chain events a year earlier. First Transformation of Genius. Then Project Resurrection of Living Presences. And now this. And Bartleby

Bratt again caught in the middle.

The peace rally might have made amends. But now—

The turbulence seemed a fire-alarm going at my ear. The clamor in the sky drowned. And I knew—the skein of my surdity had burst, I was screaming.

A gust brought the mingled smells of rocket fuel and brine— Bartleby Bratt was at my side.

"It's too late!" His voice soared over my yell.

The covey of seagulls seemed stopped in flight, then drifted in a downdraft. Then burst away on all sides.

I looked into Bartleby's face. Lines taut and scraggly chin beard soaked with sweat, he didn't have to say a word more.

The old justice's fragile gesture had proven itself futile but true. The gathering was all for naught. Titan X was not going to be launched—as a space explorer. Even the desperation Master Measure, Project Exchange of Key Public Officials, had failed. Matters between the new heads of the two hemispheres had come to that.

The covey of seagulls burst away amidst mews and mauls. Flurrying out to sea, they scattered. The firebrands seemed like no more than matches in the greyness.

The boy genius Bartleby, the beach rally, and I had lost.

We were caught in a savage gyre.

* * * * * * * * * * * * * * *

The smell of rocket fuel was overpowering— I looked past Bartleby, past the ancient justice, and across the bay. There was Titan X, clearly etched against the eerie dawn. Once our last hope, at best now an empty gesture. Three decades of international cooperation in space programs and cosmic probes were for naught. Five years of planning the first manned flight to Saturn's largest moon, now a map scribbled in sand.

Months of alternating between desperate hope and righteous concern, and now this. We should've known. Even as the joint space flight had been planned, political maneuverings put a minority party Premier at the head of the United Forces of the West. Instantly, the United Forces of the East elevated a strong man to the Chairmanship. Now two strong men bristled at each other over seas, landmasses, and mountains.

Yet we hoped, for almost a year. During the past month, our righteous concern had become troubled, even fearful. When not, we indulged ourselves in desperate levity.

We'd turned all our expectations to the launching of Titan X. So much had gone awry before, we were determined this last chance to unite the divided halves of the globe would not fail.

But now, undercut by dread, giant hope became terror.

Would the Hydrogen Missiles start flying? If so, what about the ultimate weapon, *Satan's Flying Egg?*

On exhibit in the Museum of Natural History was the reconstructed Tyrannus Rex Dinosaur. In the same room was a model of man's first anthropoid ancestor. I thought of them. I thought of them, right then.

Bartleby looked at me. Then we turned and watched Titan X as one. Over a span of five years, the multiple parts had been manufactured, tooled, and lovingly constructed, piece by piece. The joint effort was supposed to climax a generation of detente between the two hemispheres. During the past six days of the rally, derricks, blimps, and giant jets had worked as a team to set the space ship at the right angle, a mile into the sky. The special atomic engine had been raised into place in the payload capsule last, twenty-four hours earlier.

Finally ready for the Saturn moon Launching, Titan X had loomed like a hortatory finger prodding the heavens, man commanding God—Thou shalt!

Thou shalt yield us a greater place under the sun as a way of defeating the insanity of self-destruction You built into our life mechanism when You created us! Thou shalt!

Thou shalt make greater and greater room for us— Still greater room— Greater room still!— Until we have, indeed, become a little lower than the angels.

Thou shalt!

Thou shalt!

Thou shalt!

Thou shalt!— All that day.

But during the night, the derricks had been at work again. Nobody on the rally beach had dared guess what new machinery had been lifted into place.

Now, Bartleby's teen-age voice sqawking panic into my ear, I knew! I knew—

The countdown intended to launch man into the heavens toward glory and total freedom had been stopped. In its place, a grisly countdown by an iron fist toward total (and final?) war. T-V scenes of warfare fluttered in my memory— A locust plague of mordant bombers blackening a jungle village; old men, old women, children and infants, faces emptily to the sky.

Thou Shalt! now seemed a ghoulish irony.

And there was nothing to be done.

Turning as one, the demonstrators fixed Bartleby with their eyes. I experienced a flicker of renewed hope— Among them, the first of the Living

Presences, young Michelangelo materialized before my eyes. As always, he carried yard-long paint brushes, a dozen under each arm. I watched him stroke the air as though to paint over Titan X a scene much more to his liking—Jehovah's finger reaching life to the receiving finger of Adam, David's sling ready to down Goliath, and Christ surrounded at the long table of the Last Supper.

Looking in vain for more of the returned Living Presences, I was confronted by my thoughts again. *What might the mysterious activity of pulleys mean? Why had the boy Bartleby alone left the missile?*

But then I again had the feeling I experienced when young Michelangelo had appeared. Darting this way and that in the multitude, my eyes picked out the Time Machine-resurrected Living Presences materializing one by one.

As young Isaac Newton, young Abraham Lincoln, and young Albert Einstein and company emerged from thin air, I heard Bartleby whisper hoarsely, "The crew has been put on—vigil."

The inept word sounded ghoulish.

He might as well have been shouting against a harshly reverberating sky, "They have put the Cobalt Warhead in place!"

But Bartleby now standing tall again, "What's to be done?" About to bellow my agony, I was brought spinning about by a bodeful voice, "Disobedience! Pride! Arrogance!— *No good,* sayeth I." The English poet John Milton stood before me beautifully long-haired and soft-skinned in his Time-Machine resurrected youth. *"Paradise Lost!"* His voice low with this last.

I was right, in our time of great need they had returned. Their extra-sensory sensibilities turning them in to the matter between us, they gathered around Bartleby and me like an honor guard. Time Machine-resurrected at the common age of seventeen, they sometimes acted like perverse children when angry or bored and made far-flung journeyings through time and space. But always, in our time of critical need—

"If however—" Young Mohandas K. Ghandi's voice as he popped into view, followed immediately by young Mozart's, "Unless—unless—unless—" A breath of a moment later almost in chorus with young Martin Luther King's, "Inasmuch as—" and girlish Marie Sklodowska, not yet Madame Curie, "Supposing—" We turned from Titan X and looked at each other big.

We might have been holding an instantaneously stolen billion dollar banknote in our collective fingers and didn't know how to bear it away among ourselves.

Yet I was ready to go along with whatever they felt and thought through together.

In that silent second, the Living Presences were almost palpable. Young Louis Armstrong standing cornet to lip, ready—ready for the moment when he'd be called upon to outblow Gabriel himself to keep the Archangel's trumpeting from being heard (thus cancelling the heralding of Judgment Day?) If I reached out to touch him, would I feel him as substance, perhaps even as solid flesh? And all the others, too, as bodied forth living entities?

But in the moment of our sudden terror lightened by sudden hope, I dared not risk a proof of my belief.

* * * * * * * * * * * * * * *

The longer we looked into each other's stalked eyes, the more we became tuned into the hi-fidelity thoughts we shared in moments of crises. The Living Presences had—enjoyed this capability from the first when I had brought them back by means of the Time Machine as companions for Bartleby. No wonder, of humans Bartleby, alone, was tuned-in perfectly. He had to teach me the technique.

At seventeen, Bartleby was the world's leading cosmo-physical engineer. This was the direct result of my doing. I had redirected and tutored his highly fertile poetic imagination to serve the needs of the Age of Technology. The first, he was also the last of the graduates of my special creation, Project Genius Transformation.

He showed himself to be invaluable, for cosmo-astronomical engineering was found to be as much art as it was science.

I looked across the bay to Titan X again. Sprouting from the sand and stones, the machine seemed a giganticized Sequoia. Could it be just minutes before it seemed waiting to be climbed by quick young limbs, up and up into the sky, through the clouds, and farther and farther up and a-way-y-y—?

But now—

The thirteen of us made one by our shared thought, we trod single file along the shoreline toward Titan X. They trod, rather—I scurried about frantically, up and through the line from one to the other of Bartleby's otherworld companions, as a gridiron quarterback might—to reassure and, at the same time, to marshall each toward our destiny. Even as I did, young Wolfgang Amadeus Mozart swung his arms like a band-concert leader. Looking both extraordinarily sensitive and mature as though approaching the peak of his career, he had a firmer grip on our movements than I did.

I felt unsure and uneasy, but not so Bartleby. In rhythm with Mozart's swinging arms, Bartleby strode with a reassurance, even a cockiness, which, but for what I had come to know of him in the past months, might seem fool's courage. He was brash—you had to take him as that.

As for the others, they seemed, at least, to understand what had to be done. I had sufficient trust in them to put down my vague qualms. I readily assumed my accustomed role of custodian and guide as we followed after Bartleby caravan style. And I did this even though, more than ever, I had half a mind the Living Presences moved with such slow deliberation to spite me— They had paid their debt to society in lives already lived on the rack of the fullest possible expression of their genius, my bringing them back had forced them into double jeopardy, as it were. Though their natures compelled them to accommodate themselves to my project since the survival of civilization and humankind were at stake, they had at least a right to their pique, perhaps even to their personal spite. Ordinarily I would not have questioned that right. But when they acted with childish perversity, then I felt compelled to treat them as children—especially in the face of our new mission.

So, as they dawdled behind Bartleby in our fateful procession toward Titan X, I was out of all patience. Exasperated, I scurried now to one side of the line, now to the other. Sometimes, I managed to contain myself enough to walk alongside, arm against arm. In this way, we pilgrimaged toward the space ship, I acted like a seigneur who had involved the innocent in an iron-gantleted mission. But more aware and concerned than angry, I was an awkward and unsure seigneur. I was one of them, yes, but I was also responsible for them—I wanted them to know this. As such, I was more their palpitant conscience and their protector, the one who had to account for them to humankind, rather than their lord. If I showed impatience with their studied insouciance at a time of the earth's greatest crisis, let them this once indulge me. As they fleshed out into real humans, they ought, at least, to respond to my weakness humanely.

As for Bartleby, caught in the conflicting tides of his nature (self-assertion fighting instinctive reserve), he yet managed to keep his face raised high, his eyes steady and determined. He was sure of this, at least—I would tend to the Living Presences. To reassure himself, every now and again he glanced over his left shoulder.

He must have seen young Marco Polo first. The one man of action among the Living Presences, like all of them the Genovese sailor-boy had developed his special defenses against his second time around in the world of hard work and years. Ordinarily he diverted himself by affecting hot-pants now for Marie Sklodowska, not yet Madame Curie, and now for Emily Dickinson. But during the pilgrimage toward Titan X, he seemed content with checking out his current experience against the facts and events presented in the biography of his life.

Behind Marco Polo, young Isaac Newton walked so slowly he might have been bemused with thoughts of the Ur-grandparents of all of us, how they had shared a not-so-different kind of apple than the one he gnawed, and, as a result, had been forced into a moment not unlike the one he now faced.

And after Isaac Newton, young John Milton, still intoning, "So sayeth I, *Not any good!*" And, as though his personal, private talisman, the only answer he saw in the moment, "*Paradise Lost.*" I dreaded the moment he might become fully bodied forth, giving mordant substance to his Puritanical spirit. Even the enlivening cadence of young Mozart's swinging arms and the most extraordinary music he made with his mouth (like a toy string orchestra tinkling with *Eine Kleine Nachtmusik*) was not sufficient relief. For right behind the composer, young Abraham Lincoln. So gaunt and undernourished, the rail-splitter's face of pimples looked like the milky way. His eyes, so hollow and sallow they looked like twin moons behind storm clouds, he recited in a reverberating *basso profundo* long passages from *The Psalms, The Acts,* and *Ecclesiastes,* "The Lord is my Shepherd—"

Shuffling right after, young Albert Einstein. A labrador retriever shagging along on the longest possible lasso (the dog ever-circling the procession), the young mathematician-physicist slipped the leash from one hand to the other, absently. His face crinkled and vague, his expression seemed befitting a young man who, much later in life, would risk scribbling out the formula for a theory he had held close to himself since birth (why he hadn't begun to speak until well into childhood?), which theory must have been his way of making sense of himself and of all humankind standing together on the shores of the awesome vastness of the universe of infinite chaos and ageless old night into which we had all been abandoned by birth. In doing so, he had unwittingly forced all of us to share his burden and the burden of his fellow victims of genius (making us all into star-bemused Galileos, Newtons, and Einsteins)—

Relativity!

Though giving the dog ample room for its peregrinations, young Einstein held the rope tight. As though doing penance, he would help us to find reassurance in this one matter at least. Though the nature of God and the universe escaped us and we had to content ourselves with the ever-fluctuating and ever-uncertain dimensions of time and space everlasting, world without end, he had a firm grip on that dog. That, at least, was plain and certain. Let the dog circle and wind in and out of our pilgrimage line, sniffling and whining small (every now and again to release an aimless bark which sounded like nothing if not a strange contradiction of its master's famous formula, $E=MC^2$), let it yarr at me as my journey through the line moved in counterpoint, but not in antagonism to its trail.

And after young Einstein, girlish Marie Sklodowska, not yet Madame Curie. Though as thin as a flower's stem, she walked with flat-footed reassurance. Face as big as an unopened but rising sunflower and as deeply hued with concentration on the poetry of materialism, her head nodded now to the earth and now turned skyward. She seemed eternally expectant of a glowing moment of intense discovery that the sun, too, was, after all, no more than an echo of the heart of all matter, which, in turn, echoed our own heart. Our fire radiating to the sun's fire, the sun's fire radiating to the earth's! And man?—But an instantaneous echo of both the sun and the earth! And this—this, together with Newton's insight about gravity and Einstein's formula understanding, made up the *chemical* truth that was God?

Young Emily Dickinson (a frail slip of a girl who, with young Mozart, made up the most impalpable and fey pair among the Living Presences) trod with mouse-like movements right behind Marie Sklodowska. Her head nodding up and down, she might be heard murmuring as though in response to Marie Sklodowska's thoughts, *You might say so! You might say so! You might say so-o-o!*

Right behind her, young Louis Armstrong, now letting go with his firm upper lip and his pliable lower lip, in *Mahogany Hall Stomp*, to which rhythms strode young Mohandis Ghandi and young Martin Luther King (the former carrying a furled umbrella that made him look more like an English barrister than like his destined role as spiritual leader of India's moving millions, yet his eyes, as always, so direct and sage they were like two lanterns—one to show the way clearly so we might not stumble and the other to soften the way so we may continue in spite of the multitude of obstacles; while the latter looked like a photograph, handsome and open-faced, of the most-likely-to-succeed young man in any graduating high school class, black or white—no more than that, and no less). Young King strode and strode with long sure steps that sometimes crowded Ghandi's proper London-tutored walk.

And finally, Michelangelo Buonarroti, stroking and stroking with his great brushes at the towering image of Titan X against the sky to which Emily Dickinson improvised a poem—her way of responding actively to Marie Sklodowska's thoughts and, at the same time, giving vent to her own inner musings, as her eyes lowered to the caravan of her feet?

"We stand here on the strand—
The sky stands on us!
What can possibly stand on the sky?—
God? . . .
What?—
No-thing-g-g? . . ."

Her face of hardly a nose and no chin tilted expectantly up—up—only to have a view of Titan X again. Her eyes turned down to the mouselike movements of her feet as she murmured, "I don't know." Her feet moved all the quicker.

And so there they were.

And I was responsible for every last one of them. I had created Project Resurrection of the Living Presences, I had supervised the bringing of them back from their resting places in eternity, and it was my doing that they were now involved in this strange and fateful new venture—call it a crusade—which put us in direct opposition with all the established laws of our society and in defiance of the two most powerful men in the history of the world.

I was conscience-stricken that I had so involved them. My sense of guilt about them was diminished only by the sense I had about Bartleby Bratt and the terrible committment on which I had launched him the year before. Bartleby Bratt was flesh and blood and still had his one life to live—Through Project Genius Transformation, I had shown him the way that deflected him from the normal course. That I had involved myself even more deeply in each of my projects, prior to involving them, gave no relief to my thoughts—

For now, we were on the threshold of an even more portentous and fateful mission!

With the last thought, as I tried to step over the leash of Einstein's labrador retriever (just as though it were of real substance), I stumbled.

As I did, I had a glimpse of Marco Polo. Looking up from his checking out of what he read against what he experienced, he was about to make one of his hot pants passes at Emily Dickinson when he happened to turn toward the Capt. Quarter moon eyes suddenly became full and he called out, "*Vidi!*— There she blows!"

Louis Armstrong raised his cornet a mite more as though to give a riff in an attempt to forestall what might be Gabriel's premature blast on his Judgment Day horn while Ghandi's umbrella poked at Titan X as insistently as the latter poked ominously into the heavens. Only, like Michelangelo's Moses looming over the world with the tablet received from out the Burning Bush, the message of young Ghandi's umbrella seemed more like God's own, "Thou shalt not! Not! Not!"

I turned to look with all of them.

And there it was, in all its splendor of plastics, metal and turbine jets— Once the most powerful vehicle for good on land, sea, or in the air, now, with the Cobalt Missile fastened in place, Satan's Flying Egg!

Become dread, my impatience now leaped up as horror.

The moment did not seem possible. Yet there was Titan X!— No longer looking like a gigantic one, it might have been a grossly magnified artillery shell.

The bullet that might trigger the explosion of the world?

Who could say?

Who dared guess?

Right at that moment, I reminded myself again that I was responsible for Bartleby's and the Living Presences' having to face the grisly possibility with me. I had been responsible for Bartleby's transformation. I had created *Project Resurrection of Living Presences.* I had brought back the world's most sacred geniuses from their resting place in eternity. And it was my doing that they were involved in this strange and fearful new venture—call it a crusade—which put us in direct opposition with all the established laws of our society and in defiance of the two most powerful men in the history of the world.

Suddenly I was conscience-stricken that I had so involved them. My sense of guilt was diminished only by the sense I had about Bartleby Bratt and the terrible assignment on which I had launched him the year before. Bartleby Bratt was flesh and blood and still had his own life to live. Through *Project Genius Transformation* I had shown him the way that had turned him from the normal course of his life. That I had involved myself even more deeply in each of my projects, prior to involving them, gave no relief to my thoughts—

* * * * * * * * * * * * * * *

The boy genius Bartleby Bratt caught me off responses when I first—invaded his life in my special role as Guardian of the Nation's Resources of Young Talent and Expertise.

I knew he was only seventeen, but I hadn't quite expected someone so young in appearance, both short and thin.

Until he spoke, and then I heard and understood why he was considered so important a national resource. He might have been a walking library, an art museum, and (after the transformation of his imagination in the Project I fathered and directed) a cosmic physics lab., all rolled into one.

Our first meeting was in the cubby hole office he'd been assigned as a graduate assistant in the nation's leading Institute of Technology. The Atomic Research Foundation had sent me to look him over as the first of a possible army of geniuses to be transformed from the areas of their personal choice to Project Transformation of Human Resources—Space Flight, Titan X. Simply put, the nature of my mission, then, was to search out the most brilliant and promising talents in areas hitherto considered unrelated, therefore unuseful, to the Space Program, to astro-physics and technology. Such talent might best be found in the arts. My theory was that such talent, if sought out and transformed before having proved its worth in its chosen field, might provide just the inventiveness and insights that would overcome problems hitherto resistant to conventional, straight-line scientists. I guess the workings of such transformed genius would lead to breakthroughs hitherto impossible.

As an example, I used myself. Trained originally for theology, overnight I became a convert. Getting up from my study desk at the Theological Seminary where I showed promise of becoming another Tillich (perhaps even another Calvin or Luther), I decided I would redirect my efforts to New Psychology and New Sociology. Not only did I make this decision on my own, but, more, I also created the disciplines and even put together textbooks, constructed laboratories for experimentations and developed field laboratories for live research. I also supplied the awesome designations for the new fields, *Psychometrics* and *Sociometrics* for the Age of Technology. When I thought I had developed convincing expertise in the area, I offered my services to the Foundation.

In this way, I became the first of transformed talents to supply the needs for entirely untried dimensions of knowledge to solve the problems of a society rapidly entering the Age of Technology. My services proved themselves so valuable, the Foundation enlisted me as their chief recruitment officer in searching out and convincing other such talent in hitherto untapped areas such as the arts, poetry, painting, and musical composition. After great soul-searching, I finally put down my qualms enough to consent to the Foundation's request, but with one proviso—that my part in the search for talent be made exclusively among those already exposed to the climate, idiom, and procedures of technology.

Therefore, my first subject became Bartleby Bratt, graduate student in Tech. Writing and Education and a highly promising practicioner of the New Poetry. It was his talents as a New Poet that brought me to his graduate office. Like the Neo-Classic English poets of the 18th century, he married rhyme to reason and both to the imagination. I soon discovered the boy genius' talents were not merely as a creator, but also as organizer and teacher. He demonstrated fertile imagination, a surprisingly mature sense of structure, and extraordinary human insight that bordered on prescience and foresight. If permitted to flourish as intended, his talents might have produced a body of literature as promising as the early flowering and prematurely interrupted talents of the English poet, John Keats. Fulfilled, his talents as a poet might have developed a literature as great as the most mature works of William Shakespeare.

After almost a year of working with Bartleby Bratt before and then after his transformation, I became convinced of that. But by then it was too late to make amends, for in no committment to Technological Research And Knowledge is it so difficult—impossible, let's say—to turn back the clock. Even if we should make attempts by setting the hands back, we would be deceived for the interior mechanism itself, transformed to such relentless accuracy and precision, would continue as it had become.

Therefore, my sense of lost chances, of wrong efforts, of—guilt and responsibility in respect to Bartleby Bratt. I tried to make amends with a new project, *The Living Presences*, but such efforts are, at best, but salves, not cures.

The first moment I met him in his office, I should have known better. But, at the time, I felt what had proven so—rewarding a decision, so far, for myself, could be no less a promise for someone else. Even to this day, this line of reasoning still seems sound to me—in the abstract. Talent is talent, and the satisfactions for the person of talent are great in whatever area expressed. Therefore, those areas in which service to mankind is a byproduct of expressing talent must offer correspondingly greater satisfaction. Since mankind's needs were so great (defined by the ultimate question of human survival) service in the area of the Foundation's work was of infinitely more value, therefore promised greater satisfaction, than service to—the muse, as it used to be put. So went my reasoning.

But, what I did not take into account was the matter of individual inclinations. Just so—inclinations, not choice! Choice had little to do with the matter, but temperament, inclination, and the individual's bent, uses, and habits did. I soon discovered, the mind (even talent itself) might be easily transformed, but the character, habits, uses, and emotions in which the native talent has been couched was something entirely else.

But, as I say, I did not discover that until too late to make amends with Bartleby Bratt.

The first moment in his graduate office—I knew from the records the Foundation had on him that he was seventeen, but I hadn't expected so young—boyish, actually—a seventeen. He was not only short and thin, but his face showed only two or three hairs (not yet the sparse red-tinged chin beard which he was able to grow within a few weeks of entering the transformational course in the Foundation, which beard I interpreted as an attempt by his pysche and life's chemistry to make up for in physical appearance what his soul seemed to lose in wisdom). He had his shirt off, showing the thinnest and knobbiest chest and shoulders I'd ever seen on a young man. His shoulders were so knobby, they seemed actually to be trying to sprout boney wings—as though he were intended to take to the heavens naturally.

Perhaps his—boney wings contributed most to the initial impact he made on me. For in that first moment, he seemed both extraordinarily boyish and also greatly old beyond his years, even ancient (as the sages of the English Romantic poet William Blake's Prophetic Books and lithographs seemed ageless). He seemed to belong to the timelessness and sageness of the prophets of old, the thinkers and seerers of the truly great among poets, musicians, and artists.

He seemed a living embodiment of the gallery of "saints"—his "stations at the cross of greatness," as I thought of the accordion shuffle of photographs of the great which he had pinned on the wall above his desk, looking down to him from the maturity of their great achievements as though with anguish of mind and soul even as they challenged him with a single word, "Well?" Well, what now are you going to do to make you worthy of taking your place among us?

Well, when are you going to begin doing it?

Well?

Well?

Well?

I swear, I could almost hear that one word keeping at him even from the smiling faces of Louis Armstrong and Mahatma Ghandi, especially from the sober faces of Michelangelo and Marco Polo, and most especially from the severe faces of Isaac Newton and John Milton, "Well?" Maybe that's why I experienced no qualms as I approached him with my—mission—and why, too, he seemed willing, if not exactly eager, to listen when I broached the matter to him as indirectly and as diplomatically as I knew how.

As I entered his office and was confronted by his boyish but sage face turned to assess my presence over his nude shoulder, I knew nothing more about him than his age and that so far he had written but one poem that could be thought of as being both ambitious and successful, not just finger exercises as his previous efforts had been. A long poem, it was considered to be a Technological Age equivalent of the English poet Alexander Pope's *Essay On Man.* Bartleby Bratt's humanities professors and mentors in the Technological Institute considered his effort to be as successful in doing for our times what Alexander Pope's essay poem did for the 18th century. Bartleby Bratt's poem encompassed, presented, and restated in commonsensical but poetic language some of the fundamental philosophical, religious, social, and scientific questions and problems of our society. Going one better, the poem also suggested some of the answers and solutions. The demonstrated achievement of this long poem brought him to my attention. Since he had hitherto produced no more than a few hundred lyrics, sonnets, and odes, all in imitation of William Shakespeare, Percy Bysche Shelley, and John Keats, I felt justified in approaching him with my new mission cloaked under the high-sounding designation *Project Genius Transformation To Solve The Problems Facing A World On the Threshold of the Age of Technology.* I felt compelled to make at least this one experiment. When I discovered the full import in terms of the subject's personal happiness, it was too late for me to make amends with

Bartleby Bratt.

As I entered his office that first time, in addition to the gallery of "saints," I saw a babel pile of books everywhere. A multitude copies of the Bible, collections of poems (Dante Allighieri, John Milton, Goethe, John Keats, and many others), anthologies of short stories, essays, and poems, innumerable novels, and, every now and again, a tech textbook. On the walls opposite to each other, side-side to the gallery of saints, reproductions of Renoir, Tintoretto, Boticelli, Titian, Rubens, and Cezanne (the most modern). Little objets d'art everywhere.

As I entered into all this, the boy genius viewed me over his left shoulder, then swung around in his swivel chair. His deep and saturnine eyes confronted me. But only for an instant. The next instant, as though a judgment had been made, he motioned me to take the chair alongside his desk. He seemed to have a sense, he seemed to know.

Sitting down, I said, "You're the boy wonder, Bartleby Bratt."

"I am Bartleby Bratt—that's correct," his voice was as deep as his eyes, and resonant. "And you are here to—missionize my soul." And there it was, and in the voice of a much older person and one of sturdier physique.

Wanting to grin, instead I managed to respond in kind, "And you, young man, have powers—to read my mind." Then managing a real smile, "Why I'm here actually."

He smiled in return, so I broached the matter immediately.

His first response was, "But you know I'm a poet—and champion imagination over reason—"

"Exactly why I'm here," I said. "Reason seems to have failed us in solving value questions. Since New Science faces the frontiers of such questions, we are stymied—so we now turn to those, like yourself, who excel in imagination and in dealing with value questions." And swinging into my arguments, "We'd like to put you to work side by side with our amoral and—unimaginative astrophysicists. Perhaps we may so begin at long last what we should have been doing from the very beginning, at least raising, if not solving, value questions—even as we pursue scientific inquiry, experimentation, and invention. A new dimension!— Science at long last doing what should have been done from the beginning! We might have been spared so much in warfare and grisly destruction!— We might not today be on the threshold of Technological Warfare!—"

Bartleby Bratt's eyes beginning to glow, I added the clincher, "Why I—about to complete my theological studies decided, on the road to Damascus, to transform my talents, interest, and—dedications to what I call Psychometrics and Sociometrics—"

His eyes firing up with the last, I knew the first stage of my mission was achieved. I guessed the very terms I had used, *Psychometrics* and

Sociometrics, as much as my own conversion and my obvious sense of dedication, won him over. For Bartleby Bratt was that word conscious, even after his transformation.

But before he decided for the program, he had to consider his decision.

"I must first consult with my buddies, *The Living Presences*—" and there it was, the first time I heard the designation which, months later, we attached to the Time-Machine Resurrected Geniuses.

"Living Presences?" I sat back.

"Let me introduce them to you—" He looked up to the Gallery of Saints as though to a bar set in the heavens, and, with a turn of his hand, presented each in turn, "First is Marco Polo," as though paraphrasing the great Italian's own phrasing of the opening of his *Travels*. "Then, Mikey Angel," to Michelangelo. "Then, of course, Ike," pointing to Isaac Newton— "Then Johannis Miltonis, to John Milton of *Paradise Lost* and *Paradise Regained* fame. His hand holding the dour face long in range, I studied the sublime poet who had himself become transformed, into Oliver Cromwell's bitter-tongued pamphleteer, round-headed but as square-minded as anyone had ever been (would a similar transformation take place in Bartleby Bratt?).

"Then Wolf!" Wolfgang Amadeus Mozart— "Next Stretch," I smiled with surprise to his designation of Abraham Lincoln.

"And of course, Little Emily!" Emily Dickinson, of course. "Next, Ali Ein," for Albert Einstein. "Ma'am," for Madame Currie— "The Mahoot," for Mahatma Ghandi. "Satchmo," for Louis Armstrong. And finally, "Marty," for Martin Luther King. His *Living Presences,* his *L.P.*'s, for short.

His hand swept back to me, as though presenting all humankind, "Meet—" He looked at me, "You never did say your name—"

"Pro-fesss-sor Thaddeus Smart!" I said with a smile at myself.

My title was heard as I intended Bartleby Bratt to present me, yet the boy genius offered me forth as, "Tad Smart—" without so much as a whimsical smile.

"That'll do just fine!" I seconded his familiarity with an even bigger smile. "Although it's a kinder short-name than some of my friends are apt to call me, not to say anything about my—antagonists."

"Yes," Bartleby said with a look of discovery, "you look just like a—Tad Smart."

"Thanks," I smiled even more expansively. "And you, just like a Bartleby—Brat!" I pronounced it just so.

"That's o.k.," Bartleby Bratt actually winked. "I'm good at that—*epethetizing,* they used to call it."

"So, I see—" I nodded upward to the Gallery of Saints, "'The Mahoot,' indeed!"

"As for my last name," his voice became most resonant. "You needn't hesitate to use it—I took it for my surname when I discovered I was born a bastard." And then, quickly, "And now if you'll excuse me—"

"Of course—" I rose.

"I must—commune with them." I understood him to mean his piles of books and his art reproductions in addition, of course, to his saints.

"I understand—" I left the office, pulling the door tight to insure him absolute privacy, and strolled down the corridor for a peep into a classroom window, a bemused browsing of a bulletin board. As I did, I had a sense of uneasiness and of a silence that was eerie.

Whatever it was he did in his office, he did it all right and took his time doing it—I must have paced the empty reaches of the corridor a half dozen times. Finally, when he stuck his head out and summoned me back in, he was on his feet, and standing resolutely.

"The answer," he said, without sitting down, "is, I'll do it." His face to mine, his eyes held my eyes steadily. "I'll lend myself to the Project."

As he spoke, I felt a chill, then a sense of great concern—for him, for myself, for the two of us in that room—for all mankind. But I didn't then understand why. All I understood was, the moment seemed awesome.

From that moment, even though I was only five or six years older, Bartleby Bratt took to me as a son to a father. He looked up to me and trusted me. That was why my conscience began to ache so with a finger that pressed more and more during the following months. For I was awakening to the magnitude of the responsibility I had undertaken.

But by the time my conscience was alive enough to move me, it was already too late to save Bartleby, or myself, for that matter. One thing was sure, I would not involve anyone else in the project—anyone else living, that is. For this reason and in this way, Project Living Presences was conceived. It was my only way out, for once I realized the enormity of what I had involved Bartleby Bratt in, I knew no human being ever had the right, under any circumstances and for whatever noble cause, to—do this to another human being in a project of so great dimensions and implications the responsibility literally bogolled the mind, the heart, and the senses.

When I witnessed what happened to Bartleby Bratt in the months that followed, at times I felt frozen with my sense of guilt. Making the discovery too late to do anything about saving Bartleby Bratt and myself sent me to a psychiatry.

But, I must say this in my own behalf, the matter of discontinuing the original project, and then expending enormous care and at a cost of great pains to create the alternative project, the Living Presences, was entirely my own responsibility also. I was guilty in the first instance, so I felt responsible to create something as good and even better. Thus *Project—The Living Presences.*

I make this plea at the bar of history's judgment so that my - pride, derived from my personal knowledge and committment, might be judged with leniency, if not forgiven. I shall not compound my original pride with arrogance by asking the impossible, that history forget what has already been played out so far, that was hurtling toward a crisis of imponderable magnitude at present.

I'm sure the force of my palpitant conscience compelled me to go along with Bartleby Bratt's desperation plan to High-Jack Titan X to the Earth's moon and there to play out a plan which he had not yet revealed but which The Living Presences, at least, must have guessed. The stakes were that high—and my conscience burned that furiously. I had been responsible for—undoing a man's life, so to speak—I felt compelled to contribute what efforts I could to make an attempt to keep two men from—undoing the world and, if the world, the universe too? Possibly!

The months following Bartleby's decision to go along with my program, we were constant companions as I tutored him in the Foundations series of cram courses. How could I help be witness to what the transformation did to him?

The more he crammed into his brain and the more precise his thinking became and the more concrete, his imagination, the greater was his decline in other, more human areas. Bartelby grew inches taller and thinner. But it was not his thinness of body and face so much as a certain thinness of heart and spirit. Where once melancholy but warm, his eyes now became inward. As for his deep and resonant voice, it too had become thin, even breathy and spastic. The sparse chin beard, which seemed such a miracle at first, soon contributed to the aura of thinness by making his face seem oddly elongated.

More than that, the more he adapted himself to the new discipline and the more useful he became for the Foundation, the more isolated he seemed to become. In the early months, he had taken his lunches with members of the staff. But then he caught up with his teachers and soon was making his special contributions to the program, the student now becoming the leader. His inventiveness was so outrageously revolutionary, knowledge, information and techniques hitherto gathered had to be challenged. Once challenged, more often than not much was discarded. Of course, some of his colleagues were alienated, for few seemed to relish the reversal of roles which forced them to serve as laboratory aides to his creative genius.

Soon, he and I sat across from each other, alone, at lunch.

Curiously, the greater his isolation, the more inventive he became—so long as he was shown approval by the Foundation Director and the administrative staff and he was assured of my friendship. The Director and staff were so pleased with Bartleby's emerging contributions, they virtually gave him a free-hand. Which he took eagerly. The results?— The first workable Time Machine.

When Bartleby's work produced the last, the Director approached me about the possibility of enlisting still more Bartlebys in the Foundation's work. Weren't there composers, novelists, painters, they asked me, who, transformed to the Foundation's work, might have their special contributions to make that would push knowledge into still more exciting areas?

"There might be," I replied, but without committing myself.

"Well, then, what are we waiting for?" The Director rose to his feet from the conference table. "What?" One board member. "What?" Another and still another board member.

"I'd—like to take the matter into advisement," I said.

"Advisement?" The remaining members of the board rose to their feet as one.

"I mean," I rose slowly, "I want to think the matter through—" And, a lucky thought, "To devise a mode of approach."

"Well, then, do!" The chairman extended his hand. "Good-bye!"

And that, my dismissal, set me on my way.

As I left the conference room, I kept thinking of Bartleby Bratt—as he had been before I had approached him in his office the past spring (though he had been something of a loner even then yet his colleagues had spoken of him with both respect and affection), and as he had become in the Foundation. Whereas he had had a distant rapport with his fellowstudents and his teachers and seemed to like himself and was liked by others in the Institute, his work in the Foundation had set him so much apart from his colleagues a separation shut him off not only from them but also from me and, ultimately, from himself. Soon a virtual abyss yawned between us, even at the lunch table.

Especially at the lunch table.

I was concerned about Bartleby Bratt and I was worried about what might lie ahead for others like him.

Walking away from the conference room, I decided I would stop guessing and go to him directly.

At the door to his office in the Foundation, I paused. The other side of the panel, I heard Bartleby Bratt's voice, high and insistent, giving orders as to an army, "A-ten-tion!— Left Flank forward, hite!— Right flank, to the rear—march!" A moment later, he marked time, "Left-Right! Left-Right!" And then, swingingly, "Left!— Left!— I had a good job and I left!

"First they hired me!— Then they fired me!— Then, by golly, I left!"

Turning the knob, I opened the door and looked in.

Bartleby Bratt was sitting on the floor of his office. Marshalled all around him were structured models of atoms (the molecular particles painted red, green, and yellow). He was also surrounded by models of the various missiles and space vehicles which he had designed over the past few months. These were regimented forward, to the left, to the right, and to the rear in groups of fifty as toy soldiers used to be by boys a generation or more ago—in the manner of 17th and 18th century warfare.

First this regiment forward, and that to the rear—then the other forward, and this one to the rear.

And the enemy?

No regimented forces faced his armies and missiles—just the babel piles of books. As I stood in the doorway, I saw plainly most of these were textbooks, handbooks, and workbooks, mostly in physics, mathematics, and technology. Every now and again, a lonely volume of poems of John Milton, the complete works of John Keats.

"Missile regiment A!" Bartleby Bratt's voice rang out. A pause, then, "Forward—" Another pause, then, "March!— Hite, two, three, four!"

As I eased the door open still more for a fuller view, the hinges grated. Yet Bartleby Bratt seemed deaf to the sound. I looked over his desk—the Gallery of Living Presences was not in place. But what did I expect?— During the past months, he had mentioned his—confidants and companions less and less, until, his new work going apace with a high level of productiveness, he had ceased mentioning them. They had ceased to exist.

Standing in the doorway, I made a decision, brought the door closed and returned down the corridor to the Director's office. A half dozen intra-Foundation phone calls and the Director had the board gathered around the conference table.

I chose to make my announcement on my feet, "Gentlemen," I spoke slowly but with firmness. "I've made my decision— Under no conditions will I enter into the recruitment of any further candidates for Project Transformation of Genius!"

Once contained and at listening attention, the conference table fairly burst with sounds of outrage and dismay.

"However—" I raised my voice, trying to assuage the moment to orderliness again. "However—" I made still another effort. Gradually, responding to the Director's voice added to mine, the table again became attentive. "However, I have a substitute program to submit—"

"Go on, Professor," the Director nodded. "We're all attention again."

"First, you're entitled to an explanation," I cleared my throat for the explanation.

"Yes, we are," the chairman again.

"Indeed!" The board members, balefully.

"Bartleby Bratt!" I said. "But not Bartleby Bratt—" Quickly in response to their befuddled looks, "But what the transformation has done to him."

Again the table became noisy, the board members turning to each other, then to the Director, and finally back to me.

"In the past months of his training," I said slowly and firmly, "I have watched a happy and alive human being slowly transformed into a—robot."

This time the Director cried out as though grievously hurt and the board members became tumultuous.

"That's right!" I persisted over the clamor. "And I don't intend to be responsible for that happening to another human being."

"Do you know what you're saying, Professor!" The Director now joined the others in such a pandemonium as I have never before heard. I had not expected anything of the sort from such disciplined minds and contained personalities.

"The Time Machine!" I called through the outburst. "Bartleby Bratt himself has supplied the means to an alternative way—" I was determined to continue until every last one of them was listening.

"I will not recruit living human beings for Project Transformation, no," I emerged in an even and slow voice. "But there is the other way—of The Time Machine."

And so, the new project, *Project—The Living Presences.* I gave the project the designation which I knew would please Bartleby Bratt. After all, he was both the father and the benefactor of the project. I served only as the obstetrician, so to speak.

I volunteered the names of those who had appeared in Bartleby's Gallery of Saints. This, too, would please Bartleby, thus making up to him some little of the unintentional harm I'd done him.

The reason The Living Presences seemed the best alternative was simple enough in my thinking. They were geniuses, there was no gainsaying that—but more than that, they'd had their chance at life and were now physically dead therefore would not experience the horror that accompanied the transformation of living genius, such as Bartleby's had been. Also, they were Bartleby's boon companions and, as such, would give him companionship and comfort in the final stages of *Project Titan X, Saturn-Moon Landing.*

Finally, Bartleby's choices for his gallery were all good ones. They represented a wide and balanced spectrum of talent. Our work would be enhanced by their presence.

And so, The Living Presences—how they were born. How they were resurrected, rather, and why.

Bartleby took to the resurrected Living Presences as to long-lost kins. We had brought them back in The Time Machine at Bartleby's age, seventeen, for two reasons. First, their relationship to Bartleby as buddies would be enhanced by their similar ages. Second, at such an age they would serve as litmuses of the world of young rebels surrounding us. The Foundation had an ancillary idea— By observing how the Living Presences responded to our world situation, we might be helped to determine what we should value and nourish in the responses of our oversensitive and over-reactive young, and what discourage and put down. The theory was, whatever in our rebellious youths' responses corresponded with the responses and behaviors of the Living Presences was to be encouraged since history had proven the Living Presences' great worth. In this way, society would be saved from the grievous errors in judgment history might lead society to regret. In effect, by bringing back the Living Presences at seventeen, society had created the possibility of judgment by hindsight, as it were.

Both Bartleby and I had several smiling quibbles (and reservations that were not so smiling) about the theory, but we found enough of worth in the project to let the quibbles (smiling and serious) go unspoken. For we were, by age and temperament, on the side of the seventeen year olds, whether legitimately alive or just Living Presences.

The effects on Bartleby?— He responded to them as a once-orphaned boy (which he actually was) discovering that he had a family after all, and a lively, highly intelligent and interesting family at that—his own Gallery of Saints who as photographs had nurtured him and reminded him of work he was destined to do, now brought back in the flesh as young men and women of his own age.

He was obviously overjoyed. And his work showed it as he pushed on to new levels of inventiveness.

As for the secondary function the Living Presences were to serve, the Foundation and society-at-large were delighted. The resurrected people's anticipation of the responses of the world's youth was infallible.

But that was months behind us. Now here we were, facing up to our first great test. Gaining admission to Titan X and, more than that, once inside—

* * * * * * * * * * * * * * *

Bartleby Bratt gained admission to the control tower by a small ruse which, in turn, was made possible by an oversight. The oversight resulted from the force of emotions.

Until the night before, Titan X's mission had presented the crew with spacious prospects of flight beyond earth's moon to Mars, Venus, Jupiter, and Saturn (and through the gloriously multitudinous dust and meteorites of our universe and beyond (beyond our cosmos too (beyond even our galaxy (still more beyond (more beyond still)?)?)?)?)?). You can imagine Captain Valdamir Goodnik's dismay when his orders were changed to put his crew on a war-time footing. And when the International Crew realized this meant taking on Satan's Flying Egg piggy-back, was it any wonder Titan X's commanding officer was so upset he neglected to collect Bartleby's security materials when forced to dismiss the seventeen year old second-in-command because he was not quite the mandatory age for armed combat?

Thus, Bartleby was able to flash his top priority Technological Research Communication pass to the eye at the control tower peep window the next morning.

Once the door was opened to him, most of the rest was left to the Living Presences. Combining their special psycho-spirito-mystical powers with Bartleby's expertise in scientific imagineering, the Living Presences bolstered their colleague's command of the situation in stages.

Framing Bartleby from behind in a kind of greeting cards montage (rosy-faced yuletide choristers at the gates of Milord's castle) young Louis Armstrong gave such a riff on his cornet in duet with Mozart's rococo scatting that Emily Dickinson was moved to say one of her poems, made up on the spot—

"Closed doors
Needs must open,
Otherwise
Why else be
They closed?"

Reciting in so caught and dainty a voice, Emily Dickinson yet managed to make herself heard not above or against but with Louis Armstrong's cornet and Mozart's glissandoes of scats.

The moment so unexpected, the door-opener was charmed into just enough inattentiveness to permit us to slip by rapidly into the control room in our usual order.

Reinforced in this way, Bartleby put to use the Hi-Fidelity extra sensory perceptions he had learned from the sprites to dominate the personnel. Where he failed, his voice sometimes booming and sometimes wispy, the Living

Presences came to the rescue by doing their individual things, but now in concert.

Anticipating the personnel's every move, thought, and response, Bartleby managed to make each freeze long enough to enable the Living Presences to exert their psycho-spirito-mystico charisma. Hamlet-faced Lincoln looming like a human stalagmite sweating solicitation and warmth over doll-like Emily Dickinson as she improvised still more verses, Albert Einstein held the labrador retriever back like a Chinese kite caught running in a ground wind from which it wanted to rise free and soar, and soar, and soar as it was intended to do. At the same time, young Mohandis K. Ghandi swung his furled umbrella in an increasingly syncopated legato in time with Michelangelo's multiplc paintbrushes now twirling like batons to the ever-continuing and ever-crescendoing obligatto chorus of Mozart's scatting, Abe Lincoln's basso profundo oompahing and Louis Armstrong's wildly riffing cornet urged on by Marie Sklodowska's sad but knowing smile.

In this way Bartleby took charge of the control tower personnel and commandeered the communication system. But convincing Capt. Goodnik and the Titan X International Crew was something entirely else.

Searched out from the far-flung corners of the globe person by person, each member of Titan X crew had been chosen for his or her dedication to the idea of international cooperation expected to develop eventually into world order. The crew would be expected to be loyal to their original commission. We would have to convince them their dedicated purpose would be served better if they transferred their loyalties to our new project, High-Jack To The Moon.

Once Captain Goodnik had been won over, the others would follow, we felt sure of this since their belief in his judgment was that great. We made our estimation of the crew's devotion to Captain Goodnik on the basis of Bartleby's own high regard for his former commanding officer. Captain Valdamir Goodnik had been chosen from over a half thousand Russian leaders participating in Project-International Xchange of Key Personnel to command Titan X as originally commissioned. His orders changed, his mind would be open to strong influence—we were counting on this.

Bartleby Bratt had little difficulty making contact with Captain Goodnik on Interspace Communications from the control tower.

"Lt. Bratt—" the good captain's voice reverberated from the Intercom Receiver. "What are you doing in the control tower? —You were given home order, not?"

"I was given home order, yes, sir!" Bartleby responded smartly. "But that was at dawn— Now," he crackled papers, "I have new orders and most urgent ones at that!" He flashed his I.D. "You see—I have identification!" Then quickly, peremptorily, "We request permission to come aboard immediately, Sir!" As he confronted the moment, Bartleby's voice now boomed and now fell away. "I have in hand orders from our collective United Forces of the West and our remaining friends of the United Forces of the East—to deliver to you. Most urgent, Sir! Most!"

I confess Bartleby's aplomb in face of the critical moment of Captain Goodnik's belief won my deepest admiration. He was that convincing—initially—to me, to all of us.

"Collective orders?" The Intercom Receiver soared with Captain Goodnik's voice and his Ural Mountains physique simultaneously. Looming on the screen, he might have been our own Abraham Lincoln in middle age, but in place of the wart or two which now adorned young Lincoln's clean-shaven face the captain sported a flowing rope beard dangling down the Tolstoyan peasant blouse he wore at and away from work. Soaring precipitously, Captain Goodnik's voice revealed the extent to which the man and boy had shaped each other during the past months of working together. During a time of massive conformity, these two prided themselves in their ability to serve to the utmost without sacrificing their individuality. In spite of that, or because of it, they had influenced each other so greatly Captain Goodnik's inner cussedness forced him to resort to Tolstoyan affectations in an attempt to shield himself from the impact of Bartleby's personality. But with the change of orders of the previous night, now about to be changed still again, he was so shaken up he could not conceal the force of Bartleby's influence. Both hands pulled on his beard.

"Whatever can you be meaning, Lt.?" The bomming voice leaping into a tremulous tenor, the pyramidical body compensated by converging on the screen down, down until a gigantic hirsute face alone confronted us.

"Orders for immediate blast-off of Titan X for strategic ionosphere positioning, Sir!" Bartleby stood at full attention before the bristling image on the screen. Neither Bartleby nor I had ever known this angry side of "Cap'in Nick," as we sometimes called him behind his back—or "Val," our affectionate form of address.

The features on the screen grew larger and larger and fewer and fewer. Russet flop of hair and the beard, on which his two hands tugged as a deacon might the rope of a church bell, vanished first. Then, the russet bristles of sideburns and cheek hairs momentarily like stalks of wheat, his forehead and mouth vanished, leaving only the nose and eyes to fix us with their intensity. The pores of his nose showed like mid-twentieth century telescopic views of mooncraters and one hair stood up like an oak seedling in rich soil. When the left eye vanished, the screen seemed to go beserk— Only the right eye, popping blue, and the nose, streaked with veins, the nose hair now looking like a sapling.

Right then, Captain Goodnik might have been the great Cyclops examining a centipede Polyphemus minutely. The nose vanished, magnifying the eye even more.

The next moment, moving this way and that, the great eye might have been Pop Art come to life as protoplasm.

When the eye blinked, Bartleby said, "Our allies have sent envoys, carrying sealed coordinated instructions for their respective Titan X crew members." He motioned with his hand to the Living Presences who stood as tall as they knew how at attention.

"See for yourself! And hear them too!" Bartleby's voice boomed as he motioned Marco Polo to the Sending Camera.

"A Pasta Fzool a te Mom!" Marco Polo scooted to the camera and started to make a waterfront gesture. But the biography dropping from his hands, he aborted the gesture to make the recovery.

"You hear?—Italian!" Bartleby's voice soared as his face turned from the camera to summon Michelangelo urgently.

"Pater Noster—" Michelangelo stroked the screen with a brush, then a second, a third, and a fourth as he continued intoning, as though uttering an incantation to ward off Prime Evil, which, right away, set off John Milton's drone, *"Paradise Lost."*

"Church Latin—" Bartleby's voice now sounded in a resonant baritone. "Envoy from the Vatican." Face solemn, he looked into the camera directly, "And from ancient Greece!"

"Karashaw!" Captain Goodnik countered as though to fend off the moment. But then, his eye becoming but an iris, until it too vanished, his voice alone remaining whispy and thin, "All right!" And then firming somewhat, "Just because is being a Goodnik, the captain is no—dope." The shock of the slang word notwithstanding, I remembered Captain Goodnik's father had been a simple file clerk in a Kremlin office and the captain's political staunchness and his strength of character, rather than his intelligence had gained him his present position. Smiling inwardly, I managed to contain myself until I heard Captain Goodnik go on, "And you are having no right to be—snooty." With the last, my recognition of how much of an impact the boy genius had had on the commanding officer of Titan X shook loose a guffaw.

"No, Sir!" Bartleby saluted smartly as though to make up for the misunderstanding between the captain and himself and also my laugh. "I didn't want you to think—"

"Think-smink!" The voice from the Intercom boomed again. "That's being the trouble with you, Lt. Bratt—you are thinking too much!" As the voice soared with the last, my mind echoed with a follow-up line. But interrupting my inward quoting of *Julius Caesar,* Captain Goodnik's voice boomed again, now plangently, "The elevator is just now being sent down from the capsule." I watched the bloodshot eye emerge on the screen again, a moment later to become two eyes, than a blobbed face with a squashed nose. Finally Captain Goodnik himself was again recognizable.

"Come aboard!" His face retreated from the screen into head, neck, shoulders, arms and stomach. Finally the trunk, legs and feet were also presented by the screen.

And, there the captain was again, all six feet four inches of him. A towering and commanding presence with chin beard flapping like a flag in the backwash of his sudden movements.

"Pronto!" An insouciant smirk through his accent. "That's being Spanish for *On the Double*, you know!" Again, he put his eye all the way down to the set. This time it was to wink, big and deliberately.

Someone in the control room giggled nervously.

"Aye! Aye! Sir!" Bartleby saluted smartly with a click of his heels.

"Si, Mon Capitain!" Stepping up to the camera, Marco Polo saluted in a way that looked suspiciously like it, too, might have been born on the waterfront. It might have been a mid-twentieth century Marx Brothers gesture, just off the forehead, nose, and chin.

"That'sa Italiano and Franco, both!" Marco Polo gave the gesture again, "But hands, shea speak in—uni-ver-sale lang-wage!"

"Righto, Sir!" Isaac Newton up front now briskly, as though to make amends for Marco's offense.

"Valedicet, yes!" John Milton too, but dourly, *"Paradise Lost."*

"Jah-wohl!" Mozart snapped to.

"Yes, Sir!" Abraham Lincoln in his deepest adolescent basso. Right after him, Emily Dickinson in a soprano treble. And so, Albert Einstein in a German tenor and a Yiddish alto, both. Marie Sklodowska in Polish coloratura. Mahatma Ghandi, in crispest of crisp English counterpointed by a Hindi dialect, perhaps. Then Louis Armstrong, soloing in American; Martin Luther King, in American English; and finally, Michelangelo Buonarotti intoned in Church Latin, "Thy will be done!" His eyes lifted to high above the Intercom Screen.

The control tower somberly attentive by this time, I managed to squeeze in a last and least "O.K." Ordinarily I would have been furious with the Living Presences for their mild capers. As it was, Captain Goodnik apparently sufficiently impressed not to detect the true undersurface of the moment, I was both surprised and pleased enough by the results to redirect my emotions into a fulsome smile that could have been misinterpreted as a conciliatory and cordial resolve. It was not easy, but I managed to appear most agreeable in the backwash of the Living Presences insouciance. Truth to say, I actually was—when I saw the effects on Captain Goodnik.

"Will be waiting at the elevator doors!" Captain Goodnik's words sounding in our ears, we hurried for the elevator as a galvanized team converging on a fumbled ball. At the shaft, Captain Goodnik's last words reverberating still, we listened to the humming of the descending car. Finally, the doors opening, we oozed in together as one. And so, again, as sooften in the past months, though they might clown to cover up their uneasiness in the face of stress, when the chips were down the Living Presences were always perfect—soldiers, as it were—a team.

* * * * * * * * * * * * * * *

As we whirred up Titan X's launching superstructure, I had a view of miles of aircraft carriers with a multitude of escorting destroyers steaming under full power through the furrowed waves. Above, a half thousand atomic-powered bombers floated in saw-toothed clouds through which chevrons of rocket fighters wove a spastic guard, front, rear, left side and right—in, out, over and under.

From the northwest and southwest, lines of reinforcements converged, swelling the fleets in the air and on the sea, endlessly.

The landings of the temporary elevator shaft were staggered, every fifth of a mile. At each, I had views through the openings in the superstructure. With each view, the hurtling fleets on the ocean and in the sky grew larger. Soon the sky seemed a sea of milk-white, strangely afloat with gigantic silver fish and white whales while the sea was darkened with flocks of prehistoric birds, flying east, not south.

When I narrowed my eyes, both above and below long and wide dark lattice work of spider webs seemed spun link by link out to sea. In between, a helicopter hopped up and down like a water-bug caught in the countercurrents, the unlikely quarry of both until it settled to hover over the peaceniks massed on the beach.

No seagulls were visible anywhere. Nor were any other birds, vehicles, or creatures. Just the demonstrators. Like the helpless helicopter, they seemed the chief victims of the double web of air and sea.

Suddenly, superimposed on this distant view, a startlingly close confrontation with Satan's Flying Egg. Locked into place on Titan X's back with a complex structure of cantilevering of girders, struts, and braces, the cobalt missile seemed a great submarine going straight down into a prolonged dive even as we floated by straight up. As we flew by segment after segment of the metallic and plastic tube, my initial impression was entirely visual.

Titan X reflected the glory of the rising sun. Catching the reflections, Satan's Flying Egg radiated effulgently. Like a gigantic strand of costume jewelry, the missile fragmented the light's prism into splinters and shards of components. Blinded temporarily, I looked away quickly—only to be confounded with the after-effects of dots, splotches, and ribbons of colors to be seen only in the canvases of certain mid-twentieth century painters.

As we passed Satan's Flying Egg, I glanced down. Rising above and away from it, I watched the polish and perfection of metal and exterior mechanism. I had seen such intricate and finished works before only inside the finest watches, but magnified a millionfold.

I looked quickly past, way below to the beach parallel to the Cape.

The mass of peaceniks were now no more than an inkblot on the rapidly diminishing strand.

Suddenly the elevator stopped and the doors slid open.

And there was Captain Valdamir Goodnik, massive face, straggly but long Tolstoyan bears lying on his peasant blouse. His great shoulders and arms waited—he seemed an ogre ready to engulf and crush every last one of us, with affection.

Until he saw the Living Presences.

Captain Goodnik's voracious affection vanishing, Bartleby improvised with virtuosity. Since the captain and the crew had been trained in isolation for more than a year to meet any and all contingencies related to Titan X, they were not prepared to cope with developments such as Bartleby now perpetrated. None of them had met the Living Presences before, so Bartleby's task was simple enough.

Stepping to one side, Bartleby trumpeted each of the resurrected forward, "His Excellency, the Ambassador of Italy—*Signor* Marco Polo!" Striding to the fore, Marco Polo swept his four-cornered Genovese hat to his breast with bravura, a clicking of the heels and a slight bow.

"His Excellency, the Ambassador of the Court of St. James—Sir Isaac Newton!" Young Isaac Newton answered Bartleby's summons with a most gentle mannered and proper bow. Encouraged, Bartleby gained voice with the next, "The envoy of the Ancient Greecian City State of Athens and the Capital City of the Holy Roman Empire, His Excellency Johannis Miltonnis!" When John Milton stepped forward and intoned but the one word, *"Paradise Lost."* Bartleby was so heartened he fairly boomed with the next, "The President of Austria's personal messenger, *Mein Herr* Wolfgang Amadeus Mozart!" Mozart gave such a genteel and prolonged bow, both hands supporting him by the knuckles as his head touched the floor at high forehead, Bartleby rushed on to the next, "And Ambassador-at-large of the United States of America—" and, quickly, "A direct descendant of our greatest president of all, Abraham Lincoln—the Honorable Ephraim Lincoln!" The substitution of the last for the former, triumphantly.

By this time, I was seething again, but now Bartleby was the cause. Why such elaborate games at such a time? Surely there was a more direct way of gaining entrance.

But, no, Bartleby's method proved to be more than effective. It got immediate results, for the captain's resistance softened to affability which, in turn, became ingratiation just short of absolute egalitarianism. For a moment I was sure the captain would take Bartleby up in his great arms and crush the youth to himself with affection. But, no, Bartleby was permitted to continue, which he did, almost blithely now, "And his secretary, the Ms. Emily Dickinson—" He wiped his upper lip with his handkerchief.

Then, in quick succession, "The Ambassador of Germany, *Mein Herr* Albert Einstein— Of France and Poland, Her Excellency Marie Sklodowska— Of the African Free State of Liberia, His Excellency and Exalted Highness, Mr. Louis Armstrong, of American descent out of New Orleans— Of India, His Excellency Mohandis K. Ghandi— Of the NAACP and the Southern Baptist Convention, the Reverend Martin Luther King— And finally, His Holy Eminence's emissary from the Vatican City, *Signor* Michelangelo Buonarroti."

Since he was of peasant stock, Captain Goodnik was not to be won over that easily. Like all self-made men who had to live by their wits, he knew what was often presented was not what actually was. And so, now—even though the Living Presences' psychic powers enabled them to project a maturity of mien and a dignity of bearing equal to the temporary stations they assumed.

So Bartleby resorted to a grand finale, "And finally finally—last and least, therefore the most," he nudged me forward with his elbow, "Professor Thaddeus Smart, my mentor—and, you might say, my father-surrogate." He saluted me smartly and then saluted Captain Goodnik even more smartly. For a caught moment, the three of us confronted each other.

Massive face tautly pensive, Captain Goodnik seemed about to speak when, suddenly, the labrador retriever gave an irrepressible bark and leaped from Albert Einstein's side, fore-paws high, to land on the captain's great shoulders. All but locked in an embrace with the half-emergen , half-otherworldly animal, the great Russian bear of a man responded with but a single word, *"Kak?— Kuk?"*

"What?" What can this possible be being, this creature-animal?—this animal-creature?

"Kak?" The dog licked his face lavishly in response.

But only for a moment. The next moment, recovering his composure with his footing, Captain Goodnik disentangled himself from the dog's embrace and, with great strides, was soon upon Bartleby and me.

"Well, Bra-a-t!" The captain pronounced Bartleby's surname as though it were Russian, *"Brat,"* meaning brother, as he swept the youth up in his great right arm, "You are sefen-teen in the years, *da*, but you are also a man in the brain." He wrapped his left arm about me and drew me into the tangle of arms, shoulders, and faces, "And your *tovaritsch*, Pro-fes-sor Smart—as you are saying, smart too." He crushed the two of us to his massive breast. Our heads almost knocking, Bartleby managed a heroic, "I do what best I can, Val." When we were released to come up for air, we found the captain smiling big, ear to ear. And so, Bartleby and the captain *"Valed"* and *"Bra-ated"* each other a full three or four minutes while the labrador retriever yarred and yapped and the Living Presences stood tall and smiled.

All the while, the captain's left arm crushing me again, tighter and tighter as I waited dumbly and—valiantly for the moment to run its course, I surveyed the crew.

At the moment they did not seem what I had been told to expect, the pick-of-the-crop for so austere and momentous a mission as Titan's X's original assignment, which, when changed the night before, had become awesome. Something in the way they stood, hollowly, and a haunting quality in their faces (as though robbed of emotions)! I understood instantly— A crew picked for Titan X Saturn Moon-landing was one thing; transformed overnight into a crew for Project Satan's Flying Egg Alert, they became other.

Once a crew of high morale, even-minded, happy and eager to carry out their original mission, now seemed more like fat and lecherous Falstaff's demoralized ragamuffin army, "cannon fodder," indeed.

A crew so greatly disappointed might be without hope and feeling whatsoever. As such, they might respond to any strong order, no matter how despotic.

In the face of a demoralizing reassignment, they responded by being demoralized. It was as simple as that. And as disheartening.

When I turned back to Bartleby and the captain, I found them facing each other soberly. Locked in a slow and patient discussion, they seemed two demi-gods confronting each other at the boundaries separating time from space in a dimension that mingled the present, the past, and the future.

I had heard such exchanges before, during times of extraordinary crises and in the face of great disaster to a society, to a nation. But I had never before experienced such urgency and gravity expressed between two individuals.

Each time Bartleby tried to reach him with reason, Captain Goodnik protested insistently, "But I have my orders otherwise, Lt. Bratt!" He pulled at his beard with two hands as though at the rope of a church bell. I saw then the captain was as conscientious about his work and as profoundly loyal to a commission as he was cordial. He was bound to be devoted to the ideals of the original Titan X space project and, so, committed to his command. As a result, his equally idealistic crew seemed ready to follow anywhere he said. I knew Bartleby understood this because of the line of his reasoning.

Bartleby's argument was simple and familiar. There came a time in a crisis when an absolute moral stand had to be taken, otherwise no other chance might be forthcoming, moral or otherwise. During such awesome times, since the very survival of mankind was at stake, each human being, individually, and each society, collectively, had to do what each knew to be right, even though this meant going against orders from the highest source.

The present was such a time, Bartleby said. And as he said so, I felt my heart pound in my throat, in my face and in my temple.

Bartleby's manner made the moment all the more excruciating. Speaking in a voice both slow and deliberate, he punctuated the air between them with his right index finger. What he said was so obvious, a man's intelligence might ordinarily be insulted. But matters had come to such a state, whatever had been taken to be self-understood had to be spelled out on the simplest level and with the greatest patience and insistence.

I had a sense, never before had a moment exactly like this taken place. Comparisons would have to be drawn from the very beginnings of civilized society. Recent parallels might be seen in the countless millions of moments when a father undertook to spell out a half dozen basic truths to his son, just before sending him off to teachers on his first day of school. Only in this instance, the son instructed the father.

Bartleby might have been a supererogated preacher saying an archane ontology once lost in the ever-spiralling movements of man on his journey further and further away from whatever was basic to his humanity. For he kept repeating the old and simple truths and verities just as though they had never before been said and were being only now discovered. The word that recurred again and again was the simplest and the most obvious, "moral."

"There comes a time when a stand had to be taken, precluding all other loyalties, whether to country or even to—God!" This was the sentence that cropped up the most in the furrow of his reasoning. In the meantime, the Living Presences exerted gentle influence.

As for the captain, all he managed in response was the one sentence, "But I have my orders otherwise—" That was enough. We all understood what was implied—discipline, loyalties, and, above, all else, orders from his superior, who had orders from his superior, who, in turn, had orders from his—all the way up the chain of command, unto ultimate authority, the Premier of the United Forces of the West and the Commander-in-chief of the International Expedition.

And so it went, for upwards of a half hour between the two men—while the rest of us waited on a precipice. But we understood—it was the only way, otherwise how, how at all, would we even begin to undertake a task of such ominous gravity? How?

We took the prolonged agony as it was because we respected the captain's loyalty to given authority and his tenacity in carrying out a commission. We understood, we knew, only a higher loyalty and a more crucial duty would sway him.

And it was this, ultimately, that did it. Through Bartleby's simple sermonizing about old virtues, basic values, and simple morality involving the most fundamental of all loyalties to oneself and to the humankind, Captain Goodnik saw shining forth that which moved only another Arthur, Charlemagne, or Tolstoy. More than the mere survival of mankind—morality itself, being at stake.

And so, when the captain's one talismanic sentence sputtered into a single word, "But—" and his left hand was abandoned to fumble at his beard alone, I knew Bartleby had him where it counted, in his deepest values, his most enduring loyalties.

What clinched the matter was young Abraham Lincoln's act of recognition. Something in the way Bartleby had mouthed a single phrase, "a compulsion to do the moral thing" brought the young man to his full height, towering contemplatively over the International Space Crew, the Living Presences, myself, and Bartleby and Captain Goodnik—for just a moment. The next moment, he was bending with the greatest solemnity and concern to within inches of the good captain's and Bartleby's faces to utter, "You must, Sir— There are no two ways about it!"— Just as though both, not just Captain Goodnik, had to be convinced. Something in the youth's saturnine mien gave the moment such a tremulous intensity, the captain uttered but one word, a lesser good man paying his respects to a greater, "Si-ir!" As though acknowledging permission. And then, turning back to Bartleby, "All right!" And a moment later, broadside to all of us, Bartleby, myself, the Living Presences and the International Space Crew, *"Ya vas lubil!"* And, "All of you— Al-ways!" I recognized *"lubil"* as being a form of the Russian infinitive *to love.*

And I knew we had made it through the horrendous quarter hour together.

Immediately after, Captain Goodnik overflowed with good feelings, cordiality, and welcome-aboard. After all, he had been assigned to the command post of Titan X for those very same qualities. He had once read the great Leo Tolstoy had, in spite of great and enduring virtues, lacked the social graces. As a result, he had worked hard to make up for his saint's deficiency.

And so, now, "The presentation of sealed orders at your own time—and at leisure, Lt. Bra-at. But now—" He gestured to the men and women marshalled into intersecting diagonal lines, "Meet Inter-natio-nal Crew for Titan X!"

The two diagonally intersecting lines of the crew and the Living Presences converged with open arms and the biggest and warmest smiles possible.

As the two groups melded, briefly I picked out faces from the crew. They radiated sincerity and belief. The bearers of new orders released them from the iron constraints and conflicts raised by Cobalt Bomb Alert instructions.

Amidst a mingle-mangle of *"bravoes!" "hurrays!"* and *"karashaws!"* a melodious pandemonium of foreign tongues punctuated by an occasional yelp from the labrador retriever. Hand-shaking, shoulder-gripping, and bear-hugging from the crew to the Living Presences, from the Living

Presences to the crew. Among them, Captain Goodnik, Bartleby and I strode, arms hooked, faces wide with smiles.

Within minutes, a grisly juggernaut had been changed back to a democratic town meetings, poised in the sky. A Russian captain commanding and an American boy genius sharing responsibilities, the humankind again made ready to take off for the heavens on a spacious mission.

Turning from Captain Goodnik's moment of full consent, Bartleby announced our destination to the jubilant crew, "Man all posts for blast-off to the moon—the *earth's*, not Saturn's, that is."

Without questions, demures, or even quibbles, the International Crew separated from their new-found colleagues and took their flight stations.

Bartleby turned his head back to the captain and called over his shoulder, "If anyone should ever ask you, Captain Goodnik, just say—just say you were High-Jacked to the Moon." With that, he grinned big in response to the captain's bedazzled stare.

The captain's face filled with perplexity, then, suddenly opening with comprehension, he swore softly in Russian. A moment later, with a silly grin, he translated his surmise into American, "Well, I am being damned!"

"Say rather, *saved!*" Bartleby smiled full. "That is, if our mission is successful!— Then all of us will be saved!"

The captain studied Bartleby for a moment, and then, "Your mission, Lt?— Sir! What exactly—"

"Is it being?" Bartleby showed the good captain he too could accommodate himself, that accommodation breeds accommodation, that is. And then, "When the time comes, Captain— In the meantime, let's say we're sailing under sealed orders, shall we?" And finally, making a supreme accommodation, *"Karashaw?"*

The Russian amenity unexpectedly on the American youth's lips, the captain hesitated, squinted, then, finally, *"Ochen karashaw, Bra-a-t!"*

In this way, the command reverted to Bartleby.

"Commander to pilot—" Bartleby's voice rang through the spacecraft.

Finally, I sighed to myself. *The moment is upon us!*

"Navigator to pilot!" A female voice responded.

"Pilot answering!" A male's right after.

Bartleby hesitated. I wondered if he would go through with the plan after all, for he had been trained for an entirely different committment, hadn't he? During Bartleby's moment of hesitation, suddenly young Louis Armstrong gave a riff on his cornet. As he did, Marie Sklodowska regarded the oozing sounds with such adoration as she might only once again give any event or object of terrestrial origins— As Madame Curie, she might have been viewing the effervescent poetry of the tiny iota of radium she and her husband Pierre finally isolated and made palpable in the frigid shed years of laborious reducing mountains of pitchblende to glowing essence within.

At the same moment, Emily Dickinson sounded with another of her simply-laced but meaningful verses—

"The moment that is now
Has long since come
And gone
Where it shall be going—
Tomorrow?...
Today?...
Yes-ter-day —
y—
y—"

Right after, Wolfgang Amadeus Mozart broke out into an arpeggio of humming and scatting, the latter of which he borrowed from Louis Armstrong.

* * * * * * * * * * * * * * *

"Synchronization of dials for blast off!" Young Bartleby Bratt called out strong and sure.

"Is being synchronizing of dials all for blast off!" The captain echoed.

"For blast off!" tThe Navigator.

"For blast off!" The pilot.

Then, a multitude of dials-clicking moments later, young Bartleby trumpeted, "Blast off!"

"Is being blast off!" The captain.

"Blast off!" The navigator.

"Is blast off!"

"Blast off is!"

"Is!" Through the entire crew.

At last!

Under us suddenly a sound and movement such as I had never experienced before, materializing by the seconds. Growing, growing like a mountainous ocean wave, sound and movement swelled beneath us as one.

One moment we hovered over the earth, buoyant. The next, instantaneously, we were zooming up, up and away—like an old-fashioned 4th of July skyrocket, giganticized.

We might have been housed within the flaming shaft of Appollo's arrow whanged into the sky by his reverberating bow. Below us the torches diminished, until, vanished with the beach, suddenly they seemed gathered into one as our exhaust flames.

The sun emerging steadily into blazing glory on the far horizon, we were off into the heavens like Igor Stravinski's *Firebird* counterpointed, until overtaken and absorbed, by Respighi's variations on Johann Sebastian Bach's *Passacaglia and Fugue in C Minor.*

And so it was, a moment in which time and destiny had been (temporarily?—permanently?—for all time and space?) deflected from infinite spacious prospects reaching beyond the moon, Mars, Venus, and far-away dark Jupiter and blurred Saturn—and, through the gloriously multitudinous cosmic dust and stars of the Milky Way (the beach torches multiplied a billionfold)?—for a thrust, spin, and sail to the earth's moon.

The last view I had of the shore was of the multitude of protesters. Crowded on the highest of dunes, their faces turned upward toward us as though in an unvoiced common plea, they seemed to be mouthing, "YOU ARE OUR LAST HOPE!—DON'T FAIL US!"

And then, the blast off itself continuing, instantaneously ever continuing, my soul felt as though torn free from within me and left behind to float loose and aimless on the earth which funnelled away from us rapidly and far down below.

The blast off came to me the reverse of what I had expected. Instead of the sudden leap of an interminable elevator ride, we seemed dropped into a vacuum. We seemed to be going down, instead of up. Rather, one part of me seemed to be going down, while the rest soared upward—

Until I looked through the space window again and watched the great red, orange, and yellow blast grow under us like the ballooning tides of molten metal, buoying, rather than thrusting us upward. That was it, we seemed an extraordinary boat carried high on molten lava. Momentarily, everything of the earth I saw under us seemed like what I imagined the pre-terrestrial surface of the globe to have been like, molten and on fire—like the surface of the sun, perhaps.

Seconds before the earth became as thrown away from us like a gigantic fireball, I had one last clear glimpse through the space window— Fleets of battleships and bombers steaming and smoking multitudinously toward each other from all directions. Momentarily the view seemed like nothing so much as a view from a World Expo futuristic history exhibition. Then I thought of the deadly cargoes of long guns, fighter planes, and bombs.

I turned away from the space window.

As I did, I heard the mutterings of a voice on the interspace ship intercom, "How is it possible?— We have defied the earth's gravitational pull!" I recognized the voice as Ike's. Then, right after, Ali Ein's, "Yes! See, see—now even the earth no longer seems what it always seemed— Now the earth, not the moon, seems the moon." Turning back to my space window, I saw how true—the earth seemed now nothing more than a sudden moon, the moon's moon.

More than that, with each hurtling second, the former diminishing and the latter growing, our space ship loomed larger and larger until it seemed larger and more securely afloat than both.

As Marty's voice came, "There goes the earth!" we seemed so firmly grounded in space as to be stationary. Within the spaceship, we seemed the center of both the earth and the moon, that the two (instead of being satellites of each other) were our two satellites.

And the voice of Ali Ein again, musing abstractly against the obligatto of other voices on the intercom, "So, there you are— Re-la-ti-vi-ty!"

I half expected him to formulate right then, precociously as it were, the equation which in his later manhood was (conjoining with Ma'am's discovery of radium under her husband Pierre's mentorship) to set off the chain reaction of all the speculations, theorizing, and experimenting into developments, inventions, and events that led up to the Day of Decision and Judgment we were now in.

As though an echo to my apocalyptic thoughts, Johannis Miltonnis' voice drowned out Ali Ein's and the other voices, intoning, "Us, the Allmighty Power hurled headlong flaming into the ethereal sky from hideous ruin and combustion, where too long we have dwelt in adamantine chains and penal fire forged by our own arrogance and greed—"

At that moment, the view I had of the earth now was like nothing so much as one of those free expression paintings, a riot of the most extraordinary splotches of shapes and colors—a child's pin-wheel collage painting, finger paintings. At the same time, Marco's voice on the intercom spoke of the multitude spices of the orient, what the instantaneous colors must have called up in his mind. Mikey Angel's voice too, liquidy with reverence, "Such colors!— Such forms!— A Renaissance in the arts might develop from such a palette!"

The moment was given an extra twist as Johannis Miltonnis' voice droned on ecclesiastically, "At once as far as angels ken, we view the dismal situation, waste and wild—a dungeon horrible on all sides round as one great furnace flames—" The voice became dourly solemn, "Yet from those flames, no light—save only to discover darkness visible, regions of sorrow—"

Just for the infinitesimal fraction of an instant.

The next instant, the long clear telescopic view of the earth's surface hurtling away from us into masses that looked more and more like continent contours of a classroom globe, I turned the telescopic lense of my space window up full. My face squashed against the window, I looked hard down on the rounding-off object which had once been infinitely more than everything I could ever hope to know (more than the house I lived in, than the city in which worked, than the society and nation with which I was identified—at times even more, almost, than my imagination)—

I watched where the greatest and most amorphous land-contour was. The far edge of its downfalling surface seemed to be flaming, sporadically but over a great area, like little matches being lit periodically. Every now and again, a leaping tongue of fire (as from the sun's surface), but now a reality, not an illusion created by the interaction between atomic burst gigantically thrusting and devouring oxygen, instantaneous speed and outraged space.

My telescopic lense swung, and I scanned the land contour that looked so much like the USA, spotted with flames now too. The image of the spinning paint wheel vanished.

Both halves of the world showed fire. Every last one of us on the space ship knew we were witnessing from so distant and objective a perspective the first stages of Technological War I. We understood this, every last one of us.

Was it also to be total and final warfare, the holocaust?

Over the intercom I heard collective gasps, cries of outrage, and half-sounds of incomprehension, pity, and even despair through which came Emily's tiny voice, whispy, while Satchmo's cornet went as though with a trebled mute in *The St. Louis Blues*—

"I never had a brother—
Nor a sister too!—
To play small games of
Hurt and harm
As all children wont to do—
Until they vanish in—
To their acts—

And their acts va-
Nish too?
No-o-o-o!"

And, right after, the cornet still now, the small voice once more, but now resounding as decisively as it could with a "No!" That one word in itself somehow carrying as much force as the entire poem and the prolonged moaning of Satchmo's cornet, both.

I couldn't understand it, but right then as we suddenly went into an orbit that carried us into a loop-de-loop figure eight, encircling the earth, then the moon, the erupting surface of the earth suddenly left behind we were given a view only of the hard, cold and extinct surface of the moon.

A moment still later, back to earth again—first a view of one side (of unbreached land contours), then rapidly of the other (the flames spreading, even leaping higher). As we swung back into orbit of the sterile pocked face of the moon again, I understood. I understood—with the greatest impact imaginable what it all meant that mankind had been doing to himself from the dawn of his history—playing at games of hurt and harm, as Emily put it, we had done as little children do, through abject innocence.

At that moment I experienced compassion so great, followed immediately by an even greater sense of panic. I wanted to shout through the fire annealed plastic and ersatz steel walls of the space ship, through the great vacuuous deserts of outer space, and down to that subreal surface of the earth planet, "Stop!— Don't you see—"

But, as we swung back into the other side of the loop, my thoughts were lariated away from me as I had a view of the extinct surface of the moon again.

Through the mingle-mangle of sounds on the community intercom, Stretch's starved voice with the line from Shakespeare's King Lear, which he later in life said was the saddest he knew, " 'For God's sake let us sit on the ground and tell sad stories of the death of—' " His voice falling into surd emotion, I thought the finish of the line, " 'Kings!' "

And this said it most impactfully. If there were no longer any earth, all—every last word and iota of it—was gone—cities, states, and society itself, poetry, art, and even emotion. Every last bit of it! For with the thrusting away of the earth, people vanished. And when people vanished, then nothing was left!— Not even Emily's poem, followed by Stretch's interrupted recitation through the mingle-mangle sounds with the small but bell-clear voice of Satchmo's cornet muted as though through a de-amplifier but ever-going in one blues after another, nor all our sounds together could do more than sooth such an absence.

With the realization came a revelation that shook me in body and mind so greatly I trembled—

And the thought?— As we had hitherto known him, man was a schizoid animal—half creative and half destructive. This defined him on one level as much as any other definition I had read—at least in that moment of our interlacing orbit earth-to-moon, back to earth, back to moon—

For long periods of time, man had made his noble but halting efforts toward what he thought was good, beautiful, and noble (mixed with the crass, the ugly, and the selfish), only to have undone most of this in generations of destruction and collective insanity.

How else to account for what was going on across one half and the other half of the planet earth?—and for our presence in that space ship doing interminable loop de loops through a vacuum of space with the earth and moon the guideposts for our foolhardy venture?

And the most destructive of instruments attached to the nose of our ship, the Cobalt Bomb?

But that was intolerable!

And unthinkable!

We could not permit that!— Absolutely not!

And yet, we were at the moment—a stage at which every sage since the beginning of human thought said man could not conceivably find himself, poised on the precipice of the ultimate negation of not just the past and present, but also the future.

Total and final warfare! The holocaust!

Unless, we in the space ship—

The thought came as relief, but only momentarily (like a small breeze in a stifling miasma of airlessness and damp heat). The next moment, the thought, *But if!*—followed by a chill such as I never experienced before—

And that I, nor anyone else, will experience again?

Suddenly Satchmo's gravel-gritty voice, "It all de-pends on—US." The unexpectedness of the substitution of *"US"* for *"YOU"* in the mid-century popular song broke the skein of my pent-up emotions, and I laughed in a way that might, in other circumstances and in another place, have been called joy.

"It does! It does!" I shouted over the intercom to the voice sounding through the multiple levels of clear statements of greatest rationality intermingled with caught breathing, mutterings, recitations, humming music, and philosophical musings all produced by the L.P.'s.

Our moment growing into so great a sunshine of sociability and congeniality, Bartleby led the L.P.'s off for a go at fun and relaxation in the gaming room.

* * * * * * * * * * * * * * *

Just off the control room, the gaming room was actually a small gymnasium complete with a miniature basketball court (one basket), a miniature volleyball court, a pool table, and a corner of miscellaneous equipment and toys.

Bending his head to enter, within Stretch stood up to the basket, on a level with his eyes. Following on Stretch's heels, Ma'am, and after Ma'am, Satchmo, shashaying to a basketball, picked it up and tossed it to Stretch. Slowly and deliberately, Stretch held the ball over the basket, then let it fall through, clearing the net.

"Two points, man!" Satchmo shouted. "That makes you head man in this here game." He caught the ball Stretch returned to him, scatted with his mouth, dribbled this way and that, then threw the ball up and over—Stretch tapped it in.

"And two points for ole Satchelmouth!" Satchmo did capers away, around, and about, "That makes us e-qual, man— You hear ole Satchmo?— *E-qual,* he say!"

"Proclaim it loud!" Stretch said, picking up the basketball. "Proclaim it from the rooftops, the treetops, and the mountain tops!— Proclaim it now! Proclaim it then!— Proclaim it al-ways!"

"How about me?" Ma'am said, standing under the basket with her hands on her hips.

"Do you know how to play basketball?" Stretch asked.

"No!"

"Then how do you expect to play basketball?"

"Show me how!" Ma'am held her hands out.

"To play basketball?" Stretch looked at her dubiously.

"Show me how to play basketball so I'll know how to play."

"I'll show you—" Satchmo took the ball from Stretch and put it in Ma'am's hands. "Now—" He took Ma'am's hands and, with a "Ba-v-va-voom!" he shoved her hands upward. Their hands going up together, the ball flew oddly just short of the basket. Deftly Stretch tapped the ball in.

"Two points for Ma'am!" Satchmo chortled delta-mouthed. "Now you're e-qual too! You hear— Ma'am?— You're e-qual to all—man-kind!"

"But how about me?" Stretch stood tall, head towering over the basket. "I ain't sunk a basket yet!"

"Man, you're what it's all about!" Satchmo sashayed away from them toward Stretch. "You been e-qual from— In the beginnin'— And now, you is e-qual, I is e-qual, and Ma'am is e-qual too!" Then with a glance at Johannis Miltonnis who was looking at him hard, "You are e-qual! I am e-qual! He is e-qual! They are e-qual!— We all are e-qual!" He flashed a smile at Johannis Miltonnis, then turned back to the basketball game, as Stretch's voice came in obligatto, "Proclaim it loud and clear, from the aerie's of the land— We are all equal together! *Paradise Regained!*"

"A-men, Rev., ole boy!" Satchmo said, dribbling the ball.

Just then, Marco came bursting into the gaming room. Running past Satchmo, he snatched the ball, bounced it overgreatly one bounce at a time with both hands, then—swearing lustily in the half-dozen waterfront languages he had heard sailors mouth—he leaped toward the basket with both legs wide (like a frog) and pushed the ball up and over with both hands. The ball rimmed on the basket, then jumped out.

"No basket!" Satchmo yelled. "A tisket-a tasket, you did not make a basket!" He caught the ball on the bounce and threw it back to Marco.

Running about the court with the ball tucked under his arm this time, Marco dashed this way, then cut back, criss-crossing toward the basket.

"Not that way, man!" Satchmo yelled. "You ain't playing feetball!—Bas ket-ball, man!" He made a dribbling motion with his hands and then threw an invisible ball, "Hup!"

Marco pulled up next to Ma'am and then, standing like a bronze statue, pushed the ball up again, swearing as he released it, "Ah, *Bah Fun-gool!*" This time the ball went right over the basket, hit the backboard and bounced back.

Catching the rebound again, Satchmo returned the ball to Marco again, "One more try, Marco, Cat!"

But again, Marco missed—the entire backboard this time.

"Hell, man, that's no way to do!" Satchmo took the rebound again. "Here—you be referee while Ma'am, Stretch and I play one-one-and-one—why don'tcha?"

"Re-free?" Marco's eyes widened greatly, "What does this refree?"

Satchmo got set for a shot, then threw the ball up and over— Again, Stretch tapped it in.

"Two points!" Satchmo called. He looked at Marco, "That's what you say when it happens— *Two points!*"

"That's all?" Marco studied the situation a moment, then shaking his head, "No!—" And walking away, "That is not enough for Marco Pole to do!" He moved across the floor toward Wolf, Emily, Bartleby and me, hitting a volleyball back and forth over a net—two on a side.

"Volleyball, Marco?" I called to Marco. "Take my place."

"Volley—" Marco's eyes followed the ball, back and forth, "ball?"

"That's what we're playing!" Bartlbey said. "You can spell one of us at a time."

Standing on the sidelines, Marco watched big as the ball went back and forth over the net, Emily tapping to Wolf—Wolf hitting the ball over the net; I tapping to Bartleby, Bartleby hitting the ball over the net. And then the other way, Wolf tapping to Emily, Emily tapping the ball over the net—Bartleby tapping to me, I hitting the ball over the net.

In the midst of a volley, Marco shouted, "I play!" And took my place at

Bartleby's side. Again, the ball in play. But this time, when Wolf hit the ball over the net, Marco caught it and, swearing, *"Pitch-Ongool!"* walloped it with his fist. The ball leaped over the net, soared over Emily's and Wolf's head and dropped onto the pool table, sending the balls scattering in all directions and the players— The Mahoot, Marty, and Mikey Angel—too.

"Marco Po-o-lo!" Mikey Angel called at Marco with a laugh.

"Too much spaghetti!— Too many meatballs!" I called out with a laugh.

"Sphagett?— Me-e-ta balls?" Marco looked at me big. "Whatta is— New kind of confetti?— And new kind wedding dances?" Then, looking across the floor to Mikey Angel, The Mahoot, and Marty at the pool table, "What they are playing?"

Bartleby laughing too now said to Marco, "Here, why don't you be referee?— Why don'tcha?"

"Re-free?" Marco looked at him with wide eyes.

"Why don'tcha?— Watch for the ball, if it stays inside the lines." Bartleby pointed to the white lines. "If not, you call out, 'One point!' And point to the side who made the point." Bartleby pointed to Wolf and Emily. "Wolf and Emily, one team— And Thaddeus Smart and I, the other."

Pondering long, finally Marco shook his head, "No!—" And began walking away, "That is not being enough for Marco Millionem to be doing. Nowhere in book is it saying I am ever being—refree. Traveller, yes—merchant, yes—ambass and mineester, too, *si*—but, refree?— Never!" He took the biography from his pocket and waved it. "Marco Millionem is being for much bee-ger things!" His eyes became banjos. "Much—much—bee-ger things!" Wide open like twin full moons, his eyes seemed to dwarf even the basketball on the distant court and the volleyball on the near court. "Is written in this book!" He held up the book.

"You see?" He traced the title with the tip of his index finger, "MIL-LI-O-NEM!— MARCO MIL-LI-O-NEM!" And smiling proudly, "Insida, this book, she say—I am taking millionem travels, having millionem adventures, and making millionem mon-ey—millionem times!"

And, snapping the book closed and shoving it back into his coat pocket, "But nowhere—any-where—in this book is saying I am being refree for—bas-ket-balla—" He snapped his fingers at the basketball court. "Or refree for—vol-ley-balla!" He snapped his fingers at the net.

And so we played without him, until I saw Bartleby had vanished from the gaming room. In his place, the labrador retriever had appeared as though slipping through the door on its own from the control room, where we had left it with Captain Goodnik and the International Crew.

Loping from one side of the room to the other, the dog was soon a transient and honorary player in each of the three majors games and, as such, wreaked havoc wherever he alighted, furry legs, great haunches and tail and leash striking out in all directions, like a teddy bear dancing a spastic waltz on all fours.

Missing Bartleby, I stopped playing too—

Just as I did, his voice came over the P.A. system, "This is Lt. Bartleby Bratt—" He had slipped out of the gaming room and taken his command position at the Intercom Panel. "We shall reverse our engines in exactly two seconds. Before we make out approach to the moon for a landing, a few minutes to stretch our legs in outer space—for those who so like."

* * * * * * * * * * * * * * *

Apparently all liked. For both groups had their turn at a space-walk.

First Captain Goodnik and the International Crew.

Bartleby and I remained within the space ship with the L.P.'s. Our two faces pressed as one at a space window, we had a view of a sight so out of the ordinary I had to ransack my memory of scenes in art and natural science for the kinds of comparisons I needed to help me understand what I saw.

One moment, Captain Goodnik and the Crew resembled nothing so much as mermen in diving suits, cavorting in the depths of the ocean—

"Like diving dolphins—" Bartleby echoed my thought. "Or like—"

But right then I was intent on the scene. The crew seemed like visual echoes of the slowest and most legato sounds of a chamber music orchestra, in slow speed—Debussey's *La Mer*—perhaps, perhaps, Bartleby's voice vaguely in the background.

The next moment they seemed like single cell creatures I had watched through the lense of my microscope in my high school biology lab, paramecia or amoebae.

Suddenly, Bartleby's musing voice brought me spinning around to him, to what he was saying—

"Scattered, on the charred beach, pieces of wheels, blasted houses, splintered trees. Nude, I stand in the ocean froth next to an oversize wooden shell that looks like and is a decoy for a giant turtle . . .

"Now I have it clear—"

I knew I had to hear Bartleby out in the dream that had haunted him since his realization of the implications of his decision to permit the Foundation to transform his genius. As the responsible party, I had to hear him out. He was determined to unburden himself by making me share in it, and I was galvanized by my own sense of guilt and by his growing knowledge of that guilt.

"I find myself on a South Sea Island." For the first time in months his voice resounds in a modulated baritone. "A last testing of the decoy, I push the machine lovingly with my own hands into the waves before me . . .

"In deep water, I look back—the natives, then smoke from the beach-wood fire, and finally the jungle trees diminish against the horizon. Every other stroke, I give the decoy another shove ahead.

"The waves are not yet great ones. Rising and pounding the machine, they are just enough to make my movements tortuous. Hovering a hundred feet ahead, the giant sea turtle has not seen me yet. A few more feet, a quarter of the distance more—then to climb into the machine.

"When I crawl into the machine, I feel as though inserted into a sounding cave. My head sticks out easily and I am able to move about freely. Twisting my head, I look over the whitish waves to the right and the left—I can no longer look back to shore. My easiest view—directly ahead.

"I make out the turtle's head. Skin folded back upon itself withdrawn protectively within, the head points at a lazy angle from me, drowsing—before the mists lift and mid-morning heat boils the waters' surface.

"My hands and feet working with frogmen paddles, I know I can approach the turtle within inches if I move carefully.

"As I list and float, the turtle looms once again as large as the decoy machine. Now there is no mistaking it for a giant moss-streaked boulder or a round-headed dingy, nor even a Civil War steam battleship."

As Bartleby's voice droned, I had a sense— Turning, I saw Stretch listening, his face even more saturnine as he slouched, a full head shorter than usual. And Johannis Miltonnis too, nodding, nodding, as though in confirmation of Bartleby's dream. And The Mahoot, Satchmo, and Marty, the silence of their listening as deep as ante-deluvian history repeatedly reborn in the past, now being reborn still once more.

"I make out the lines in the turtle's shell where the years have accumulated into more than a century, time annealed into time into time—"

I looked away from Bartleby for the remaining L.P.'s. But for Marco, who was again buried in the pages of his biography, all the others—Ike, Wolf, Emily, Ma'am, and Mikey Angel—were at space windows. Viewing the scene playing itself out in space, every now and again one and then another turned to us and, their eyes wide like miniature moons, listened to Bartleby's nightjourney into himself.

"As I float toward the turtle, my adversary looms over the decoy machine—" Bartleby rushed on as though realizing he had repeated himself. He was aware, I was sure, of the Living Presences, that some time or other at least one of them was listening.

"A growth of barnacles and thousands of indescribable parasites on the cross-hatched under-shell. Flippers are wrinkled and overlapped—like—like uneven armor segments."

I saw that Mikey Angel was listening at that moment.

"Lolling lazily, eyes stare dully ahead—the turtle is asleep.

"I retract my arm, feeling within the shell I finally have the stick and bring it out with its noose dangling off the end like a doubled flag. I open the noose and hold it high, waiting.

"The pole of the stoutest bamboo, the noose of braided oil leather runs through loops down the length of the wood like a fishline off a reel attached to my body, just so.

"I had hoped my adversary might be a big one, a real giant—"

Now Johannis Miltonis turned and listened greatly. I tried to think what his thoughts might be but always came around to his poetry.

"As I advance, the waves toss me against the turtle, then wash me back. A sudden large swell, and I might—

"But I maneuver carefully until, pulling up alongside, I lie like its twin. I watch the head— I watch the vacuous eyes as slowly I approach, closer, even closer.

"At the left flipper, I raise the noose high above the turtle's horny head. Suddenly I have a sense of panic— What am I doing in such a hunt?-- So far out of my depth!

"I have the noose poised like a—halo. A second more, and I will drop it exactly. Timing is of the utmost—to keep the turtle from coming alive from its sleep—otherwise—

"A wave rises beneath me, rocking me forward, lolling the turtle's head. I calculate—the moment to strike will be between the swells of two waves.

"Watching, wondering if a light might flicker in the eyes with a soundless cry before succumbing, I wait—"

Turning, I saw all the Living Presences were watching and listening, but not with wonder or even curiosity, but with recognition.

"'Now to do it—' Shouting, I drop the noose over the head and about the neck, yank the stick, and watch the noose close like a hangman's knot about the neck. My hand jumps as though someone has yanked the stick, and I know—

"The instant I strike, a wave breaks under me, carrying me high with the turtle, then—washing back—dropping us against each other in the hollow. As the boards crack under me, I fight the pole frantically.

"Still I watch the turtle's eyes. I am sure they flicker, but as I yank the noose, no light is visible. The turtle has been carried over the rim of sleep into unconsciousness with my first yank.

"As I yank again and again, convulsive reflexes wrack the turtle—flippers and head thrash like the mandibles of a giant crab, tipping its shell.

"Another wave swells under us— Lifting us high, then crashing us against each other. The machine crunches under me and I feel cracks going up the belly and down the back.

"I give the pole still another yank— The head shakes with convulsions.

"I let go of the line, letting it run out.

"As the turtle thrusts across the waves out to sea, I float willessly after the line, then drift back shorewards. At regular intervals, I yank the pole up, snapping the line. The resistance on the far end carries the impact of a sledge hammer.

"Each time I yank the line, a wave swells under me. With each wave, the machine surges forward, then is dropped into the afterswell. Each time, the boards are wrenched and shattered under and above me—my left leg hangs through greatly, my right shoulder and arm are entirely exposed.

"When I finally let the line run free, the turtle hurtles far and away, farther and farther out to sea—until I can barely see its hind flippers.

"Desperately, I snap up on the line. Then again, and again. As I do, the split hull of the machine widens. Almost falling out, I cling desperately.

"What will happen when the line plays out to the end and the turtle continues plunging out to sea?

"Releasing the pole, I draw my arms and hands into the shell and feel for the reel. The leather binding has tightened in the water and the knot is unyielding—and I have no knife with which to cut myself free of the throng.

"Weary of the struggle, I look over my shoulder— The shoreline has disappeared. Not even the tops of jungle trees are visible. I go at the cord desperately— Still, still no use.

"I look out to sea—now even the turtle has vanished. What will happen when it submerges?—

"As though an echo to my thoughts, I feel the line snap taut on the lolling poll. The machine and I, with it, are pulled up, almost out of a bursting wave—a moment later to be dropped crashing against the hard surface of the water. Right after, a series of quick, sharp bumps smash the machine away from underneath and around me—

"Suddenly a lull! The line slacks before me again and the machine tosses freely on the waves— Thrashing, I manage to keep afloat amidst the debris.

"In the seaward distance, for a moment I again see the turtle, only a glimpse. The shell is tipped sharply, hind flippers in the air—head and front flippers submerged.

"For seconds the turtle floats oddly on the waves, this way and that. Then, like a torpedoed ship, it tips up, head high—hesitates—then slides under.

"The line slackening, I float aimlessly—

"But only for moments. When the line becomes taut again, I know— Soon the weight of the turtle is at me, down-dragging—and, for a fraction of a moment, I too am held aloft— A moment later, I am falling as though dropped, engulfed on all sides by overwhelming tides.

"Experiencing a panic so great I shout out—literally!—"

"What happened then?" I looked at him, yet fearful of his response.

He looked back, "You saved me!— Remember?" And, in response to my befuddlement, rapidly, "You woke me up— The morning of the day we resurrected the Living Presences, don't you remember?— I had overslept, the first time in my life I can remember ever having— The day of our work at the Time Machine."

I remembered then, all right, and with a sense of relief as deep as the sighing of blood— How could I forget, he had kept calling the Time Machine a *Plastic Womb*? I had done him that good act, at least I remembered the look in his eyes as he realized I had awakened him, that he had actually been asleep.

And now, feeling easeful, I glanced through the space window. As I did, my fingers worked the knobs of the telescopic lense, giving me a view distant beyond the space walkers. Fascinated by the sight of great leaping flames, I was sure the lense was trained on the sun. But the lense clearing, I had a view of burning cities, dog-fighting planes and flaming bombers. Massed fleets of aircraft carriers and destroyers throated shells and torpedoes at each other.

And I knew—

Again, I thought of music as visual echoes of the sounds, but now of the most violent and disjointed nature. I thought now of Igor Stravinsky's *Le Sacre De Printemps* as my view of the planet earth surged and thrust with flames and clouds of smoke. I thought of the atonality of Schoenberg too, and of what might follow in terms of the monotonality of Hindemith.

The three views seemed to class in vision and in memory, co-mingle, then break up—a moment later to co-mingle again.

Suddenly I remembered clearly, the morning of the day we resurrected the Living Presences. I had, indeed, heard Bartleby cry out in his sleep and had awakened him. Once he had been fully awake, I had asked him if he was so tormented as to have nightmares so real he actually cried out during dreams why, then, did he permit himself to be used as he was by Project Transformation, by society, by myself.

"Why?" he had fixed me with a deep glance. "Because I am committed to do so by my genius as an artist, even though now transformed." With the last, I had to look away from the agony in his eyes.

So it had been that morning, months earlier. But now, a new night dream of art, music, and humanity suspended in outer space between planet earth and satellite moon, the nightmare of an overburdened and deeply troubled soul, and the grisly reality, outdoing even a nightmare, unfolding on planet earth's surface.

And there was nothing I personally could do!

I turned off the telescopic lense. The scene in outer space emerged again, legato— Bartleby and the crew, male and female, turning and tumbling like mermen and mermaids in a watery picnic.

I could hardly wait when we would have our turn, the Living Presences and I.

When Captain Goodnik and the crew reentered the spaceship, we did not wait to hear their joyous expostulations of the dimensions of their play outside all space and time, of their excursion into the ocean of spatial eternity. We had watched them and seen! Now we wanted to know!

Exchanging no more than grunts, we climbed into the discarded space suits, waited impatiently in the outer chamber for the trap doors to slide open—and then, one after the other, as in a procession of celestial pomp and circumstance, walked with great legato strides out into space.

As we did so, behind him I was aware of Captain Goodnik and the crew members watching us at the space windows as we had earlier watched them. We, now, outside all space and time, the immortals—while they, once again within the world of the space ship, simple mortals.

How can I say how it was to us?

Now afloat, now tumbling legato, down, down, and down—and now soaring up, up, and up—and around, around, and around! As in the slowest of slow motion. After each other, under each other, over each other and all around each other as in a marvelous game of tag, ring-around-the-rosy, and leap frog.

That's how it was!— With the labrador retriever, as fully suited as any of us with a hooked-up intercom built in, serving as the—frog we all took turns leaping.

How best to show how it seemed?

We might have been a herd of elephants wallowing in a common jungle bath, a family of hippopatomuses afloat in a great lake. We were like a family of muskrats cavorting on a landslide into a great limpid pool of our own millenium-long making, while above us the labrador retriever barked us playfully on.

The labrador retriever considering whether or not to join in, we felt like ducks, drakes, and geese fluttering up and around a favorite swamp habitat, like eagles circling a Rocky Mountain aerie.

The dog most serious now, we soared like a flock of heavenly creatures determined to prove our worth for a place in the astronomical scheme of things—we, a new Pleiades; the dog, a constellation unto itself.

We were angels returning from the depths of our rightful home under the reformed leadership of the Archangel Lucifer. The dog was an escaped guard at Hades' gates.

We were heavenly choiring angels.

We felt like extensions of God Himself, that was it.

We seemed like God. We might as well have been God for we moved through space as God might have moved.

We acted like God.

The sensation was like none I had ever known. Yet, as a boy, I had had dreams of flying through space with freedom, smooth and slow, above all the world, invulnerable to any of its impediments and harms.

But the moment was also the view I had of the others so levitated. All of us seemed as if we were dreaming at one and the same time. We might have been sharing the same dream sequence together, the sequence of my boyhood dreams. There was one difference—the labrador retriever's romping through this dream made our experience unmistakably real.

I had a view of Bartleby Bratt and each of the Living Presences in turn. Then of all of them and myself, together. In constant touch with each other and with the space ship too over our space intercoms, we could not only see each other but hear each other too.

I had a view of young Ike. Even in the space suit, he seemed like nothing so much as an Andrea Del Sarto fresco of a levitated friar (surprised and titilated with the knowledge of his extraordinary powers). At the same time, bemusing his knowledge of the apple he was to watch fall to the ground in his later life, his face was pressed to his visor as though pixalated with incredulity that he was not hurtling down to planet earth or, at least, crashing against the side of the space ship. Every now and again, he triggered his space suit jets for a lilting flight—and smiled, big.

And Marco, from his visor his eyes rounded wide-open. He seemed determined not to miss anything of the norths, souths, easts, and wests of celestial journey. Every now and again, his eyes turned downward within. I knew he was consulting his LIFE again for confirmation. When his eyes reappeared at the visor, they seemed gigantically puzzled, also bedazzled. How was it possible no such glorious journey had been appointed for his actual life? How?

I turned away from those eyes.

Right then Johannis Miltonis was intoning a poem so lugubrious and slow I knew it could be only one he had written in the dark and dour days of his old age and blindness.

I turned away to Wolf and was rewarded not only by a partial view of his face but also of his furbelows and tight britches. When his face managed to appear at the visor full, it seemed a placid blank.

His voice over the intercom was something else, however. I was delighted by an extraordinary sound of Mozart's arpeggios and thrills against a monotone humming I associated with the musical compositions of Schoenberg and Hindemith had they decided to collaborate in doing a tone poem together.

And so as Mozart's small face now appeared and now disappeared at the visor, I listened to a most extraordinary musical melange. Suddenly little Emily's invisible face mad itself felt with the saying of a new poem. At the same time, young Stretch's saturnine and rocky face fairly burst against its visor as it recited passages from the Bible in a most melodious and melancholy basso while Satchmo's cornet took one low *E*, then a high *C*, followed by a low *E*, again a high *C*, again and again and again.

One moment Stretch's voice:

"In the beginning was the word,
And the word was with God!—
And the word was God!"

The next moment, followed, and in the same saturnine basso, by

"How beautiful are they feet in sandals,
oh lustrous maiden—"

While little Emily's voice improvised still another poem—

"God!
God??
God???
God!!!!"

The faces of Ma'am, the Mahoot, young Marty, Ali Ein, and Mikey Angel were full against their visors, their eyes wide. All but Ali Ein's, and his were full but cloudy. At the same time, Mikey Angel twisted slowly this way and that—upside down—rightside up—sideways, this way—sideways, that way. His right hand rose every now and again as though to dab with an invisible brush at one of the upside-down Living Presences. He seemed determined to paint them over too, to make them float on their sides and upright, adorned in splendid gowns and crowned with nimbuses. The labrador retriever too?

Right in the midst, Bartleby Bratt strode with as grand a movement as any managed by the Living Presences—

Jesus and the Disciples of the Cosmos at a First Supper!

In that moment.

As I watched and as I listened, I thought of sound so full and sonorous not even a millionfold pipe organ going against the multiple downgushing of a Niagara Falls could render it metaphorically.

It might have been the sound and sight of the universe turning eternally upon itself, grinding out its works, identities, and truths with each iota of movement and sound, motionless, timeless, and endless.

Music of the Empyrean and Celestial Chord.

Free-floating as though both a part of and apart from the moment, I knew this. I knew this. I knew this.

And Bartleby Bratt was the living nexus of the moment.

Universal Harmony, that was it.

World without end.

Amen.

While on earth—down—down—way down below us, the multitudes seemed frozen in adoration.

I bumped against the side of the space ship.

* * * * * * * * * * * * * * *

Within, I threw off my helmet and leaped out of my space garments. Taking deep breaths until my stomach was settled, I strode this way and that, so getting the feel of my legs again. Bartleby removed his helmet and jet suit as quickly, gave a great sigh and wobbled on his feet. Finally, in full charge of himself again, he stepped big to the control room entrance.

The Living Presences seemed just as happy to be breathing and walking about normally.

Like Kayoed fighters brought back with douses of cold water, we did wobbly capers through the passageway into the control room. Like the drowned recently resuscitated, we stumbled toward the crew. Walking in and out, before and behind, we surrounded Captain Goodnik and the crew. But for a few moments away from our space walk, we acted as though returned from lunacy which, in a sense, we had.

At the same time, accompanying Satchmo's cornet riffs, now silvery and now golden, and Little Emily's extraordinarily inspired impromptu verses, words meaning no more nor any less than themselves, we exercised our voices.

The moment seemed an epiphany, almost.

"A most unusual experience." Ma'am sounded almost schoolmarmish.

"Almost pukey, too—literally," Little Emily interrupted one of her verses. The moment burst, she brushed at her blouse briskly. Apparently she meant *literally* literally.

I permitted myself the luxury of a grin, but then was pulled back to reality. Something had changed in the space ship. While we had been out gathering "polka dots and moonbeams," the command of the spaceship had reverted to Captain Goodnik. I saw this in the crewmen's taut, rigid faces. Mostly I heard this in Captain Goodnik's voice.

"Lt. Br-r-at!" Bartleby's surname sounded an affront, even obscene. Soaring to his full six feet three, the captain fronted us massively. His face like a fighting rooster's, he belched, 'You be so advised, the command of this ship is being returned to Captain Valdamir Goodnik—" He poked his chest repeatedly, "To me! To me! To me!" With a sweep of his open massive hand, he took in both the crew and the Living Presences, "You hear-r-r?—All?"

"But Val—" Bartleby began—

"Don't being *Val*-ing me, you hear-r-r?" Captain Goodnik rose on the balls of his feet. His shoulders hunked formidably like a bull's, "I am being Captain Valdamir Goodnik. Captain—Val-da-mir Good-nik—First!" he pointed the great index finger of his right hand. "Second!" he added the next finger. "And Al-ways!" he marshalled forth the remaining fingers of his right hand with the reinforcement of all four fingers followed by the oddly bowed thumb too of his left hand, "Always!" And then sweeping about to the entire space ship, "You hear-r-r?"

As one the International Crew responded, "We hear."

"And you?" He looked Bartleby fiercely in the eye, right eyeball to left eyeball, his own left eye half closed. "And you?" He swung the googling right eye about, "And you?-" From one of the Living Presences to the other. "And you?"

Knowing the Living Presences were accustomed to no treatment other than the kindest and most respectful regard, I rushed in to rescue the moment with a tentative, "We hear." None too soon, for Marco was bristling.

Still Bartleby, "Captain Goodnik—Val—"

"*Nyet, Val!*" Captain Goodnik roared, showering spittle, "*Captain Valdamir Goodnik!*—On-ly!—" And then quickly, "To you!—You hear?" His right eye fairly popped as his left eye squeezed closed.

"I hear!" His voice modelated, Bartleby's words seemed as impactful as Captain Goodnik's. "But if you would only listen—"

"Listen?" Captain Valdamir Goodnik is having to listen still more?" The hirsut giant bent way over to Bartleby, put his cheek flat against the boy genius's and held him eyeball to eyeball. No looking away this time.

"Be reasonable—Commander Goodnik!"

I looked at Bartleby quickly. Rewarded by the thin undersurface of a smile, I fought my own smile.

"*Commander* Goodnik is it now being?" Captain Goodnik's eye fluttered. "Now, promoting me you are being?"

"I'm sorry—Captain Goodnik."

"Ah, Captain Goodnik?—Captain Goodnik is now listening." Captain Valdamir Goodnik rose to his ful height. "Spik!" Both eyes wide open.

"That you have a right to be revolting—" Bartleby began in what I knew was intended as empathatic speech.

"Revolting?—" Captain Goodnik's shoulders hunkered in outrage as never before, practically swallowing his head. "Look who is being calling who revolting!—It is *you, you, you*—Lt. Bartleby Br-r-r-t-t—not Cap-tain Val-da-mir Good-nik who is being re-volting!"

"You misunderstand my meaning," Bartleby reverted to his own speech pattern. "I mean to mean *rebelling*—"

"Revolting?—Rebelling?" Captain Goodnik agitated both his hands. "Whatever word, it is you—not Captain Good-nik—who is being."

"You're right, I am revolting—" Bartleby looked down at his feet. "Even Little Emily knows this." And then looking up, "You are right, the command of this spaceship is rightly yours—there's no gainsaying that. And I—not you—are in rebellion."

As Bartleby Bratt launched himself, I saw Johannis Miltonis' lady-like face lift. He seemed listening with his ears, eyes, nose, mouth and total being. I had an insight—Johannis Miltonis recognized the moment as one of conception. An idea was being born. The instant was one of divine invention.

And the rest of us? We took our cue from Johannis Miltonis' response.

Buoyed by our intense interest, Bartleby pleaded his case. Now reasoning, now arguing, then insisting, demanding and begging at one and the same time, he finally emerged smoothly in what was entirely his own voice and style. He was eloquent because he was at once dynamic and contained.

Bartleby Brat's final triumph was more of oratory than of reason or logic. The persuasive swing of phrasing and rhythms matched the inventiveness and variety of his choice of words which were both concrete and suggestive. The firey suggestiveness and exactness of his figures of speech combined with his unabashed indulgence of old-fashioned rhetoric carried the hour. I knew this, I could tell from the light that managed to glimmer in Johannis Miltonis' face.

Bartleby Bratt brought off a rhetorical *tour de force.*

But how was Captain Valdamir Goodnik to respond when the verbal fireworks were all over? This was the crucial question.

During Bartleby's opening, Captain Valdamir Goodnik interrupted with "*Nyets!*" followed by a "*Not so!*" an "*On the contrary—*" a "*However—*" "But—" "Unless—" "If—"

Finally puffing out, he tried desperately to recapture the hour with an abrupt about-face to the forcefulness of his original stance. But this time only an "Au contraire—" emerged. We recognized this as a sign of his having acquiesced, though not yet given up, to the force of who Bartleby was and the import of the moment.

What won the day was Bartleby's determination to pursue morally-overriding questions over the rights of command aboard a space ship. Authority and morality at odds, he was wedded to the latter.

But there was an extra dimension, of speech and style that made the final difference.

Calling up Marco Polo's travels to Tartary, Cathy, and the golden realms of Kubla Khan, he tapped the splendor of bountiful goods and sumptuous silks. He evoqued the flavor of priceless spices. He summoned up images of mountains of precious stones. He recited the wisdom, the sagacity, and the serenity of the Orient. Borrowing THE LIFE, TRAVELS AND ADVENTURES OF MARCO MILLIONEM from the phrase-mumbling, round-eyed Genovese, he read copiously from that book, Bartleby did.

Rounding out this segment of his oration, he concluded, "Consider the Cancellation of all this. Then consider what is at issue here."

"And gunpowder, too—Don't forget gunpowder!" Captain Goodnik interjected gleefully, as though calling out, "Check!" in a chess game.

"And gunpowder too," Bartleby bowed his head. But then quickly raised his eyes to the captain's and continued," And the holy grandeur of the paintings and sculptures of Michelangelo Buonarroti—Think, just think now—The Moses, the David, the Pieta, the Last Supper, and the Sistine Chapel—all as if lost to us. Only think—"

"You just think, not I!" Captain Goodnik shouted. "I, Captain Goodnik, is being socio-economic realist, not feudalistic ecclesiastical apologiest—"

"It was Mikey Angel's art work, not his religion or politics, I meant," Bartleby said in a most quiet voice.

"Politics, smallatics!" Captain Goodnik snapped his fingers. "There is no art without politics—without economics, neither." He wagged his index finger under Bartleby's nose.

Turning his nose away from the shaking finger slowly, Bartleby went on, "And Christopher Columbus—though he is not here and of this company—just think, he might as well have not discovered the great, then-unknown land today even greater and now known as America—"

"Goodbye Columbus!" Captain Goodnik's nose drew back and upward. And that was all he said and did, then.

"That might very well turn out to be," Bartleby began in a soft voice. "But given one more chance, we might be able to hail, '*Hello, Columbus!*' And that is what I am pleading for, that one more chance. Wouldn't you rather say, 'Hello, America! Hello, Europe! Hello, Asia and Africa! Hello, South America! Hello! Hello!'?"

"Good-bye!" Captain Goodnik belched. Then, right after, bellowed as though a basso profundo in *Boris Goudonov*, "Good-bye!" He fairly spat fire with the last, brimstone too, if you like.

"Say, rather, Hello!" Bartleby continued his recitation through the captain's continued yarrs and belches of *Good-byes* like a worn-out needle stuck in an overplayed record. "*Hello*, to Ole Ike—his theory of gravity and all his treatises on science, government, and human morals and manners. Say *Hello*, *Hello* to Johannis Miltonis and his sonorous organ-rocking poetry—" he gestured to the boy poet who, of all of us, seemed most moved. "Say *Hello* to *Paradise Lost*, *Samson Agonistes*, and *Paradise Regained*, too, *Hello*—Say *Hello* to Wolf and his quartets, quintets, sinfonias, concerti, symphony after symphony after symphony, and to his operas, *Hello*. Say *Hello*, *Hello* to—"

And so Bartleby's orotund recitation went, evoking the great works of the Living Presences all of which but for some of those by the hand of the boy Wolf still lay ahead of their Time-Resurrected ages of 17. In obligatto, Captain Goodnik's voice still counterpointed, "Good-bye!" or, as a change of libretto, "*Nyet*! You hear me, '*Nyet*!' I am saying. Captain Goodnik is saying, '*Nyet*!'—In thun-der-r-r!" He might as well have been vetoing a Security Council vote one vote short of unanimity, "*Nyet*!" The word reverberating through the reaches of the control room, the entire space ship shook like a faulted tuning fork.

Still Bartleby pursued. Resorting more and more to recitation, he quoted reams of *Paradise Lost* and parts of *Samson Agonistes* too. He evoqued the grand design and orotund tones of the former and projected the dark tragedy of victory through defeat of the latter. Then he quoted from Emily's dainty poems. He quoted real ones she wrote in her maturity, now stored on printed pages, not the verses she improvised on the extraordinary pilgrimage.

From Emily's poetry, he turned to Stretch's campaign speeches for a seat in the House of Representatives, his debates with Douglas, and finally the *Emancipation Proclamation*. Quoting the last in totality, he closed with an *Ah-men*.

Then he turned to Ali Ein, to some of his notes and letters to his wife. He read scraps of comments the surd genius of cosmic mathematics and relationships wrote on the margins of his student quizzes and papers. He also quote the straightforward which accompanied each comment, which statement was also always hedged, even, sometimes, undone absolutely by hidden reservations—for everything, after all, was relative to something else, therefore there could be no absolute *ipso facto* or *therefore*, *thus*, *and so* to any reasoning, no matter whose, even Ali Ein's. As Bartleby quoted Ali Ein, I suddenly understood why such reservations made upon reservations in so unfailing and repetitive a manner should make him seem as much a happy prisoner of an ever-evolving circle as was his head in the nimbus of white hair—world without end.

And then, to Ma'am, and to her husband Pierre Curie, too—He eulogized the example of their life together which resulted in the inception and grand birth of the finest of their offsprings, radium reduced from the womb of pitchblende.

And after, the example of the Mahoot's life, a million times repeated in the swarming millions of India. And Marty's life, too—and his tragic death. Bartleby evoked the splendor of the mornings stars of their examples shining, shining in the heavens of the hearts of multiple millions of their people in India, in Africa, and in America and elsewhere.

And finally, finally Satchmo—First way down low and blue as blue can be, A flat blue, E flat blue—Then high, higher, and higher still to clear C, still clearer C, C clearer even still until an extraordinary, almost inaudible tremolo of high D—even higher E—highest—And suddenly, rapid piano finger blues again, the ebony blacks mixed with the ivory whites. Yet Satchmo, never to be outdone, blowing still harder and harder still on his cornet-now-become-a-full-throated trumpet to give any Gabriel, Angel or Devil, a run for the show—*Blues to Midnight!—Blues Through the Night!—Blues 'til Mornin'!*—Blues! Blues!—The St. Louis—Chicago—Watts—Selma—New Orleans and New York Blues!—*The United States of America Blues*!

Yes, Sir!—Yes, sah!

The Great All-American Become World-Wide Blues!

The United States Of The United Nations Of The World Blues!

Ah-men! Ah-women! Amen!

Suddenly, Bartleby said softly but firmly, "No man has the right to cancel out all this by mere duty and loyalties what-so-ever. If you prevent the moment we are approaching, you would be negating not just the moment but everything that has come before to lead up to this moment—"

"Ah hah!—That's being exactly it!" Captain Goodnik, triumphantly. "We would not!—You would not!—And I would not have now to—"

"But don't you see?—You can't cancel out everything that has already been and all that now *is*. Why, that would be playing—"

"Bog?" Captain Goodnik's eyes googled as he supplied the Russian word.

"That's right."

"Like being playing—"

"Like playing God!" Bartleby brought his face close to the captain's. "That's exactly right!"

"Ah-ha! Ah-ha!" Captain Goodnik strode big. He pointed his right index finger at Bartleby as though he, now, had his opponent where he understood him.

Bartleby didn't say a word for minutes as Captain Goodnik continued to point and to stride. But the moment Captain Goodnik ran down, his face empty, depleted of all animus and counter-arguments, Bartleby took command of the moment, "All right!" And I understood. In spite of his Marxist dialectical materialistic logic, Captain Goodnik was still a God-Fearing man. This, not Bartleby's socio-historic cosmopsychometric oration heavily larded with references to truth, beauty, art, and goodness (all freighted with quotations, recitations, and evocations) did it for Captain Goodnik. It made considerable material difference to him that God might have stooped to manifest his will, as He might have been doing at that moment, through a creature as lowly as man or that such a creature should be so arrogant and prideful as to take on the prerogatives of Deity, idea or reality. For Marxist though he might be, he was also Russian—and that made the difference.

"All right," Bartleby pursued his hold on the moment. "Shall we proceed with filling you in on the exact nature of the plan? Shall we?—" He rolled out charting paper onto the planning board.

Experiencing mixed feelings, I moved in to the long conference table. As for Captain Goodnik, he again retreated to his expression of dubiety. His right eye wide-open, the left eye squinted. Both eyebrow soared high.

Among the L.P.'s, for now only Marco showed interest in the moment. A chart after all was a chart, nautical or not. Besides, we were again taking turns at the interspace telescope.

As he bent to the multiple viewers of the interspace scope, both his eyes resembled the captain's right eye. They were round as telescope lenses.

The moment upon us, Bartleby turned the master knob until all the lenses were trained at the same spot on planet earth. The distance and direction dials so indicated.

"Here take a look for yourself!" He stepped back from the master telescope viewer, as though inviting us as one.

As we put our eyes down to the multiple lenses, feeling as one, we saw as one whatever Bartleby's adjustments of the knobs presented.

"First, the battlefronts!" Bartleby's voice overriding our views.

It was astounding, the atomic-powered telescope brought us down into the thick of jungle warfare. We had a view so close, I, for one, could almost smell gunpowder and feel the recoil of howitzers and rifle fire. We might as well have been junglefighters ourselves.

A score of paratroopers were caught in a crossfire between opposing long-range artillery as they confronted a pocket of enemy paratroopers yards away. Every now and again, in the eerie silence between two barrages of howitzer shells coming as though in response to each other from opposite directions, one and then another of the paratroopers risked rising for a burst of his automatic rifle across the yards of grassland and brushwood at the opposing paratroopers. Each time, the scene was repeated on the other side so that every time a paratrooper rose an opposing paratrooper rose too at the same moment—and the two fired away at each other, at exactly the same moment. Each time, at least one, sometimes both, fell under the fire. And so it went, at the exact fraction of a second in between screaming howitzer shells. Every now and again, one of the howitzer shells came out of rhythm, catching the paratroopers on their feet. The result was often horrendously appalling— Again and again I pulled my eye up from the viewer as though jabbed not only in the eye, but in the mind and in the heart and stomach. At such time, some of the crewmembers looked haunted as their dazed eyes met mine.

Yet we always returned to the viewers.

Adjusting the master viewfinder, Bartleby presented us with a scene of a half hundred junglefighters dressed in uniforms recognizable as those of the United Forces of the West. Then adjusting the knob a mite, he gave us a view of another half hundred junglefighters in the uniforms of the United Forces of the East. The distance between the two groups was a matter of yards of grass and bushes, trees and rocks, yet the impression was one of two opposing armies fighting the entire war out in the few hundred square yards of jungle, that the entire fate of mankind was, in effect, being decided between those two pockets of junglefighters. Calculating quickly, I estimated if the present rate of attrition continued, a fighter or two lost on each side every hour or so, with the help of the howitzers and long-range artillery the two groups would wipe each other out within a week, if not sooner.

Bartleby manipulated the master knob quickly, wiping out the view we had for the fraction of a moment, the next moment to bring our view zooming down, to zero in on still another and another and another pocket of embattled men, each as young and as terrified but desperately determined as the first. And so it was, wherever he trained the multiple interspace telescope.

Until he gave several other knobs careful turns. Then, our view was of a multitude of fighter planes at each other in the air like lofty echoes of the multiple pockets of jungle fighting. A moment later, we watched fleets of bombers lumbering across the skies above both massive continent-groups toward each other, passing each other like fleets of freight trucks on the same highway, going in opposite directions—and, but for the sporadic fighter attacks, continuing on without interrupting each other with so much as a—wave—to unload their deadly cargoes as designated on headquarter battlecharts (those that managed to get through the swarms of pestiferous fighters)—a factory town wiped out here, fields of corn, wheat, or rice there; now a reservoir and now an atomic power plant. And this, then, was what the new kind of warfare was to be?— A stand to the last between a multitude of pockets of enbattled junglefighters while bombers carried out strategic selective bombing with the greatest deliberation, limited and contained—to avoid what both sides dreaded, Total Technological Warfare.

I looked up from my telescopic viewer to Bartleby. As we shared our horrifying thought, he looked away quickly and adjusted the master knob.

I looked back into my lense, sharing the collective view— A forest of steel.

Bartleby cleared the view—presented a scene of a thousandfold missiles ready on their launching pads.

Some of us looked up quickly.

"Ours!" Bartleby said, then readjusted the knobs again.

We turned back to the lenses— Again a view of a thousandfold missiles on their launching pads, just as though the scene had not changed in the least.

"Theirs!" Bartleby's voice overrode the moment. Yet but for a difference in the design of the shells, the missiles might have been manufactured in the same factory as those we had been looking at moments earlier.

"Atomic warheads!" Bartleby said in response as more of us looked up from our lenses. "Both sides!" He adjusted the knobs again, "Now look!"

We returned to our interspace telescopic lenses. The view now was of a score or so considerably larger missiles, also prodding the heavens from launching pads.

"Ours! Bartleby's voice again, the view clouded, blotted out, then began to reform until, clear again, a duplicate of the former view, but for minute variations.

"Theirs!" Now all of us looked up from the scene as one. I saw my anguish repeated in each face, but for the captain's which was empty as though stunned.

"Hydrogen warheads!" Bartleby said, echoing all our thoughts. "The biggest, but for the—" His voice vanishing momentarily with the phrase we all held away from ourselves, I escaped into my private thoughts. If warfare can be carried out with such grimly controlled determination as we have just viewed—like—like two skillful boxers trained to the very bone and nerve fiber of their physiques so that responses become mechanical—jabs, uppercuts, and left-hooks responded to, automatically, with jabs, uppercuts, and left-hooks pounding away at each other until, efficient and relentless attrition, breaking each other down, then at some point in the breakdown of the defenses of either or both fighters someone, or both, was going to throw a haymaker—someone would trigger the atomic missiles, and these once launched, then trigger the hydrogen bombs, and, finally, perhaps in the onrushing chaos and terror, the ultimate weapon would be sent flying.

It was this realization, then, that had led to Bartleby's formulation of the desperation plan. At least, this is what I understood.

Bartleby standing aside, I took over the master knobs and spun them until I had a view of the junglefighters again. Adjusting one of the knobs rapidly, I had a single face alone in focus. A youth—could he be more than eighteen?—his face showing hardly a beard, unmarked with experience yet wide with determination that showed terror beneath as he jumped up to take his turn at firing across the yards of noman's land at another youth who might have been his twin.

Still another twirl of the knob, followed by adjustments on the half dozen or so remaining— I had a view of a scene I hadn't even thought about since leaving the planet earth hours earlier— Armies of rebels setting fields of wheat, forests, and buildings on fire. Sporadic uprisings here, there and everywhere, in the West and in the East. While a highly disciplined and controlled series of jungle wars were going on according to clockwork, revolution and civil war was springing up spontaneous and spreading like wildfire, literally.

I pulled my eyes away from the telescopic view—the lense remained wide-open with the scenes, repeated multitudinously in the other instruments.

Taut with terror, I faced Bartleby as did the others, stunned with attention.

"This is the rationale of the plan!" Bartleby began slowly and deliberately, pulling us in together over the blueprint he had stretched across the planning board. His eyes held the captain's, then travelled to the eyes of each crew member, settled briefly at rest on mine, then return to the captain's. As he presented the plan, his voice and his demeanor grew strong to the echoing responses of the Living Presences and myself. I could only guess at Bartleby's scheme, but the Living Presences freely giving support was enough for me to yield him belief.

The blueprint stretched across the planning board was actually a solar map—the sun centering up the orbitting planets, each in turn orbitted by its satellite or satellites, and all these in turn positioned in the cosmic dust of the Milky Way. So the map was actually galaxial, and more.

In spite of its grand dimensions in space and scope, Bartleby treated the solar map with such detailed attention, detached as it were, the design might as well have been an atomic magnifying glass photo of an atom, blown-up a billionfold. He might have been briefing a class in neuclear physics.

Curiously, the studied coolness of his manner made the presentation all the more excruciatingly terrible for me. As for the others—I dared not look at them.

"A given number of gravitational vectors of masses of solids and gasses will always, through multiple levels of interaction through billions of milleniums, arrive at an equilibrium beneficial to the totality. Such a balance results from a infinity of ever-continuing adjustments, arangements, and rearangements among all component parts in relationship to each other and to the totality. Through this process, the totality makes accommodations to this planet cooling off so many degrees with each passing millenium and that one gaining so much additional weight or another losing such weight as the result of the activity of meteors, asteroids, and comets entering from outside the solar system or hurtling away from the solar system. Thus ever-so-slight changes in the established order are accounted for through a billionfold multiplicity of dynamic adjustments—through space without end and over time without beginning or end.

"And so it has been for unaccountable billions of aeons, and so it might continue to be for still more unaccountable billions of aeons— So long as whatever changes that take place are not so large and so abrupt as to make adjustments impossible!—" His voice stopped, abruptly— I felt such a start in myself and in the crewmembers around the table! Captain Goodnik looked up from the solar map, as though his head had been yanked— His eyes were agaped as though struck with a rock.

"Perhaps—" Bartleby's voice soothed the moment, "Perhaps, the sophistication of this balance between changes and adjustments as established within our own solar system, the refined marriage between dynamic energy and ripened harmony is what characterizes our solar system most and makes it possible as the place—perhaps the only place—where that most wondrous of all cosmic event, the birth and sustenance of life, is made possible, on the planet earth." He looked up from the solar map with his tracing finger on the orb which was the planet earth.

"But supposing—" lifting his finger, Bartleby looked about the crew from the captain to each man in turn. "Supposing a massive and abrupt change were threatened in the solar scheme of things." As he said it, flatly, he looked away from the crew and the captain too, to the far empty side of the space ship.

"Supposing—" his index finger spotted the earth's moon, "the moon was transformed into a space ship that could be jetted out of earth orbit—randomly into space?—" His eyes came back and hooked the captain's eyes briefly. The moment between the two men was horrendous. Bartleby looked away quickly back to the far wall.

"Rather, supposing we project this possibility to the two warring sides on planet earth—as a threat—blackmail, if you will—to force them to their senses—

"Supposing we did!"

The impact was all the greater for Bartleby having presented the possibility as an imperative, not a question.

"And if they are calling our bluff?" The captain yelled, and seemed surprised to hear himself doing so.

"Then—" Bartleby snapped the moon out of the design and sent it flying at random through the length of the space ship, across the room, into the long corridor down its length, and away.

As Bartleby snapped the orb out, all of us including the Living Presences were startled dispropotionately as the structural design of the solar system fell apart before our eyes. So innocent and inevitable a happening yet also, in the metaphorical moment, so awesome to our view!

"Only," Bartleby's voice came as a dubious rescue, "with the jetting of the moon out of earth orbit, the effects would be equivalent to the fission of a giant atom, leading to a solar chain reaction— And, if solar—then galaxial— and if galaxial, then cosmic— And if cosmic—"

"Enough!" Captain Goodnik leaped before him, his legs astride and his arms flung out. His massive face worked with anguish and his eyebrows fluttered as he clenched his fist as though to retaliate to multiple blows upon his person and those for whom he was responsible.

"So you see!" Bartleby's voice came so still I could hardly hear him even through the vacuum of absolute silence that envelopped us. "They must not call our—bluff!" And then, his voice full again as he faced up to Captain Goodnik tall and forthright, "Besides, what we present as a threat may be no less than what lies ahead for all of us anyhow—even if they do not call our bluff and we do not carry out our plan— For what we threaten them with is only what seems the inevitable outcome of the technological warfare on which they are launched—the Hydrogen Holocaust. No more, nor any less!"

The last, again one of those excruciating phrases.

"Our hope is they will see our threat as such," Bartleby took command of the moment, "no more nor any less than a dramatic projection of the outcome of the road on which they have put us—that one way or another, if they persist in the war, the solar system (and, if the solar system, then—)—"

The outcry was so terrible, I knew instantly only the Living Presences could have produced it. Like the inaudible scream of Picasso's *Guernica*, it seemed to come from neither man nor beast alone, but from an anguish-annealling marriage of their souls by an event so horrendously aweful the two had been reduced to some infinitely more human than the humans and at the same time more primal and primitive than the beasts of the mural.

I knew instantly why they cried out so!

Having lived out their natural lives in the pre-technological era, they had not, as we had, been preconditioned by infinite gradations of exposure to the possible inevitability of the atomic holocaust. With this realization, I felt as conscience-stricken about the Living Presences as I had hitherto felt about the transformation of Bartleby Bratt. Suddenly I knew, even as I had no right to saddle living artists with the burdens that accompanied the transformation of their geniuses to the uses of humankind, so was I wrong to have tampered with the fragile geniuses of the spiritual world. Bringing them back to live through and respond to the problems of the world of technology, after they had already served their own ages, did them a great violence. One time around as a palpitant genius was enough for anyone. More than that, to compel them to live through what man has made of their genius was to force them into an atonement for sins not of their own doing. Neither Ike nor Ali Ein, nor even Ma'am, were responsible in any way for the manufacturing and dropping of the first atomic bomb—why should they be forced to agonize through the consequences?

As for Johannis Miltonis, Wolf, Emily, Stretch, the Mahoot, Marty, Mikey Angel and even Marco, in what possible way were they personally implicated by their acts or the nature of their genius?

As I lashed myself with my conscience, Bartleby Bratt's voice sounded through strong, growing even firmer, "This threat becomes our tool for working good— The combined power of our Titan X atomic reactors and the neuclear force of the Cobalt Missile, when engaged simultaneously (the atomic reactors at full acceleration the moment of detonation of the Cobalt Missile), would be sufficient to launch the moon on a random flight through the solar system, a gargatuan spaceship run amuck in the universe, as it were.

"The likely outcome has just been demonstrated—" His putting the matter so impersonally made the moment all the more excruciating.

Again, a collective tremor so great followed, everyone of us felt it— Bartleby plunged ahead with the moment in full command, "What we need do now is to convince both the Premier of the United Forces of the West and the Chairman of the United Forces of the East that we are fully up to resorting to such desperate measures!— We need to communicate to them the magnitude of our sense of desperation!— As for the rest, earth scientists will convince them of the dimensions of the power we have at our fingertips.

"We must communicate our determination not to settle for anything less than a sane solution to problems through a cessation of hostilities, with the view in mind of working out a *modus vivendi* toward such time as we are up to living side by side and amongst each other peacefully and justly."

With that, Bartleby swept each of us with his farouche eyes. And then, through the tension that was like torture prongs in our nerve ends his voice nudged at us quietly, "Gaming anyone?" Just as though great events had not been unfolded for our examination, ultimate questions not posed followed immediately by an ultimate answer. Right then, I understood—Bartleby's great capacity as a leader revealed itself most through just such touches that turned the portentous and imponderable into manageable matter.

Feeling the tension already lifting, the L.P.'s and I fell in behind Bartleby single file as he crossed the control room and went out into the passageway that led to the gaming room. The crew and Captain Goodnik remained behind at the controls.

As I left the control room, I had a fleeting sense of something being not as it should. Glancing back over my shoulder, I saw what it was—the labrador retriever was not accompanying us to the gaming room. Instead, at one of the space windows he gazed out into the eerily swirling cosmos of swirling stardust, an occasional meterorite on a random flight through suns, stars, and planets, and the scattering of configured constellations here, there, and everywhere across the heavens.

Almost certain I saw longing in his hirsute face, I turned my attention back to my colleagus and walked after Bartleby briskly.

* * * * * * * * * * * * * * *

In the gaming room again, the L.P.'s turning to their usual preferences on the miniature basketball and volleyball courts, at the pool table and on the floor beneath, Marco reverted to his usual smiling roll, "Inna book is saying, amma big man with millionem wo-men." His smile glinted, taking in both Emily (at the volleyball net with Wolk, Bartleby and I on the other side) and also Ma'am (already at her basketball game of *ménage á trois* with Satchmo and Stretch, one x one x one).

Settling on Emily as his initial target, Marco began moving in like a prowling wolf. Upon her, he was about to touch her when, from the opposite court, Bartleby hit the volleyball over the net. A ball flying at her, Emily jumped up (right out of Marco's hands, as it were) to tap the ball to Wolf, who sent the ball flying back over the net. The ball coming at me, I gave it a bust up and over the net, returned to Wolf, who now tapped it to Emily, who, in turn, sent it back over the net to Bartleby. And so the warm-up went, back and forth—with Marco left standing with his arms empty.

Suddenly emitting a spate of *bah-fungools* and *enfant chiens*, he turned and, loping like a wolf, started to descend on Ma'am. It was time-out on the basketball court. But as soon as Marco hoved into view swooping down on Ma'am, Stretch called, "Time-in!" And the three began dribbling and sinking baskets, one-one-and-one and also as a team of three—with Stretch always held in reserve to sink a basket whenever Emily or Wolf failed.

Swooping down on the basketball court, a flying leap away from frail Emily, Marco came to an abrupt stop. Panting for breath, he considered the situation and, apparently, considered himself too. For when he began to move again, his approach was both graceful and slow. Advancing foot by foot, padding like a cat, he began reciting—

"*Si come il sole*
Che si stesso egli
Per piu litizia
Come il caldo ha rosa— "

Almost upon her, he reached slowly to take her thin white arms, gently, in his hot hands. Giving him an open and wistful smile, she said, "Why that's from Dante's *Il Paradiso*—" and in a small and fey voice translated freely, "You say, if God is

> "Like as the sun
> Which burns in noon's sky
> Giving too much light—

Then I am

> Like breath of roses
> Rising, rising
> Unto you—
> Singing this song."

Marco's hand about to close on her arms, Emily stepped lightly away from him, "But that is sacrilege, Sir!— Dante says that about God, how it is to look on His face and how then on Beatrice's face after, not on an ordinary lady's." And, with an afterthought, "Even Beatrice is supposed to be a—figure for the Virgin Mary." With that, she served the volleyball lightly over the net. The ball coming to me, I was about to return it when Bartleby hit it out from my hands. The ball leaped up and over the net, and went soaring halfway across the gym floor.

"One point for Emily and Wolf!" I called out. "Wolf and Emily are ahead."

"Why, we're ahead!" Emily clapped her hands and jumped up and down before Wolf. Each time she jumped, she moved farther away from Marco's still grasping hands.

Not to be daunted, Marco approached again. But now in movements of greatest legato and sounding with an opera aria, in a high and vibrant tenor,

> *"Che gelida manina—"*

"That's from an opera— Don't tell me, let me guess!" Emily put her little hands up as though to fend him off, "But that was composed after your time, how is it—"

"Since being brought back, amma reading books, no?" Marco's hands reached slowly for her frail wrist, "I have been listening to re-cords too—to Gigli," his face moved closer, "To Caruso—" still closer, "To Mario Lanza and to Sergio Franchi, to—"

Bartleby sent the ball hurtling over the net at Emily. As with a will of their own, Emily's hands thrust up to tap the ball to Wolf, who sent the ball back over the net in a high arc, suddenly dropping to the floor to ricochet out—

"Point for Emily and Wolf!" I called out. As I did, Bartleby turned on with a scowl, "Where were you on that one?" Hitherto I had seen only Johannis Miltonnis scowl with such intensity, and then on the rarest occasions and when muttering, *"Paradise Lost!"* mostly. For a moment I had a sense, I was seeing a side of Bartleby I had not known before, and plainly. In that moment, I felt both shame and compassion for my ward— He was of a mind to participate in the special world of the L.P.'s, let him! Hadn't he always communicated with them as though they were his playmates, his bosom companions? But that was before we had brought them back by the Time Machine. Since then, I had watched him become more and more eager to be with them, to be like them, to be *one* of them, actually. He had come to feel so like one of them, he responded to them as he did to his own kind, to human beings. That is, interacting with them, under stress he projected his own mortal emotions (of competition and ambition, for instance) on their immortal world (disturbing its equanimity, as it were). I saw this in my moment of revelation, that his failing was not that he wanted to be one with the L.P.'s, but that he wanted to be what they were and still remain what he was. He wanted to eat his cake and have it too, as it were.

This, I knew, was both his greatest flaw and also his dark glory. He wanted to become one with the immortals while still remaining a human being, therefore mortal. As for myself, I was content to be both human and mortal and, as such, felt out of the moment completely.

With the realization (the score: Emily and Wolf, 5—Bartleby and I, 2), I walked away from the volleyball court to the pool table. The Mahoot, Marty, and Mikey Angel were deep into a game of Eight Ball. On the floor, underneath, Ali Ein sent a yo-yo up and down while Ike watched the goings and comings of the spinning plastic disc, down to the floor, then just short of hitting, spinning back up the string into the air and Ali Ein's waiting hand. As Ali Ein sent the yo-yo on its journey once more, he said abstractedly, "You see—Re-la-ti-vi-ty!" While Ike kept muttering, "So there you are—Gra-vi-ty!"

Right at that moment, I turned to look back at the volleyball game as though yanked, for Bartleby was trumpeting his displeasure he not having scored once even to Emily's and Wolf's twice. As I glanced, I saw Emily tremble ever so lightly. And it was this that made me see the moment of Bartleby's exposure most clearly—Though the size of his mind and his talents made him like one of the immortals (shown most by the work in which he was engaged in the Titan X Project), he was still only a mortal, subject to all the frailities of human flesh and blood, of the human heart and ego too. It was this that set Bartleby and myself apart from the Living Presences, nor matter how much we shared of their company and no matter how close a rapport we established with the[illegible] As fully as we thought we knew them and shared their thoughts, we could never by any stretch of the imagination or effort make ourselves over so as to become one of them—not while we were still living, that is. Our passions, our ego, our wish, hope and dreams (as I often put it) which compelled us to yearn to be of their company were the very matters which stood between us, separating Bartleby and myself, human flesh and blood, from the Living Presences, pure spirits. I knew this, and this was my saving grace. But as yet, Bartleby did not. The trouble was, during the past months of our association, a subtle change had come over the Living Presences. As Marco, Wolf, Ma'am, Satchmo, The Mahoot and the others had shared our lives, they had adapted themselves to our ways, and, doing so, had even come to like some of our customs and games. As right then, the games of basketball and volleyball, pool and yo-yo. In this way, though immortals, they had become humanized and, thus, sometimes acted like human beings. The two romantic triangles that were developing, for instance—and Marco's attempts to break into both triangles so as to claim Ma'am and Emily for himself. For Marco was out to claim some of the rewards the book claimed were his, women being the chief among these. His tragic flaw, his pride, as Johannis Miltonis might put it was considering himself worthy of so deep and devoted a love as Ma'am's and so delicate and fragile as Little Emily's. In this way, Bartleby and Marco were like each other, each in his own special pride. Were their tragic flaws those of attempting more than they were able to accomplish with value. Perhaps?

I wondered about this right then. As I did, Johannis Miltonis muttered dourly enough for all to hear, "Vainglorious pride! Arrogance and greed! Beware! Take care!" The seventeen year old youth's voice was bodefully doomful. How dare anyone presume to try to change the delicate modes of relationships established over the centuries of those who were literally just a little lower than the angels. Johannis Miltonis' judgment fell as heavily on Marco as on Bartleby. For each—immortal and mortal—was committing as large a sin in terms of his particular modes of behavior.

Though I might not agree with the young roundheaded Puritan's judgment, I yet understood it. His definition of what was awry seemed to make sense. For Bartleby's insistence on relating to, thus intruding on the serene world of the Living Presences and immortal Marco's ardor to make immortal Ma'am and immortal Little Emily part of his conquests was as good a definition as any. For Marco's vulgar overtures to Ma'am and his seductive approaches to Little Emily must have reminded Johannis Miltonis of the archtype of all evil, the Primal Serpent. Either Ma'am or Little Emily could have been Eve.

"Of man's first disobedience and the fruit of that immortal tree!" Johannis Miltonnis' voice rose, and shaking his right index finger, *"Paradise Lost.* Yes! Yes! And Yes!"

Escaping to the sidelines, I made my way to the pool table. But the voice pursued me all the way, just as though I were the accused. I became overattentive to the activity on the pool table—The Mahoot, Marty, and Mikey Angel still making their trials and errors in a game of Eight Ball. I watched them sink the eight ball again and again before its time before they finally managed to run off a proper game (as the Mahoot put it). Still they approached the game slow and slow— How else to restrain the overzealous Mikey Angel's great sculptor's arms from wielding the cue stick like a gigantic chisel? Finally, a—proper run-off managed Mikey Angel seemed to lose interest—

Until, his turn to break, he flourished his cue stick with such virtuosity and power and drove the cue ball with such force the rack of balls virtually exploded in all directions. The balls slammed against all four sides of the table and then (rococheting off each other, this side of the table, that side of the table, the top and the bottom, with such a clicking and clacking of ivory never before heard) one after the other dropped two by two into the four pockets, every last one of them—and in the correct order, the eight ball last. The cue ball now alone on the felt, still bouncing off one side and the other, Mikey Angel grinned big, gave his cue stick a summary flourish and, was about to lay it down on the table, when the cue ball, too, disappeared.

The Mahoot and Marty gave a gigantic groan. Still grinning, oblivious of anything but triumph, Mikey Angel laid the cue stick on the felt and sat down on the floor next to Ali Ein. The spiralling and jumping yo-yo seemed to intrigue him enough to challenge his attention for minutes.

But minutes later, having mastered the spin sufficiently to make the wooden toy return up the string to his tuggings, he put the yo-yo down too. What to do?—

Next to the pool table, a pile of building blocks, clay, and finger paints waiting on the floor. Ahhh!

I sensed, rather than heard Mikey Angel sigh. He was a painter, yes, and a sculptor, yes too. What was to prevent him from trying his hand at architecture? What?

But, not architecture alone!— A multi-media art which combined painting, sculptoring, and architecture!

Ahhh!

Now he distinctly sighed aloud. And as he did, he strode across the floor and sat down again, amidst the building blocks, boxes of clay and bottles of finger paints. Within minutes, he had a construct rising from the floor. I watched the building build, block set upon block, clay for the insterstices, and scenes painted on the sides of each block.

Suddenly, seeing the construct as it was intended, a most extraordinary cathedral with uncountable multiplicity of spires soaring above an infinity of apses leading out from a great circular nave, I said aloud, "A space chapel!"

And so it was! Here, on the floor of the gaming room of Titan X, Mikey Angel had finally taken the opportunity to build what he must have yearned to build all his life but had found humanly impossible—even for the great Michelangelo Buonarroti—an entire cathedral with his own hands.

It was a great wonder. And even he knew that it was, for he kept standing up and away from the construct, to admire his own work. Each time, he smiled pleasure and expressed satisfaction. The great painter and sculptor who had never been able to find complete fulfillment in his life's work seemed now to be doing so—at play.

Reflecting Mikey Angel's new-found contentment, I smiled benignantly.

In the meantime, above, the Mahoot and Marty ran off still another rack of Eight Ball with smooth skill. Marco's seductive poetry and song ever accelerating, Emily and Wolf had drawn so close they scored again and again off Bartleby. The score surging ahead in Emily and Wolf's favor, Bartleby became all the more desperate to score and thus was soon fairly cannoning the ball in every direction and to the far reaches of the gym. And this whether serving or returning a serve.

Now that Johannis Miltonis had returned to dour surdity, I watched and listened. I had a view of Marco surging on his toes. Raising his right arm with taut index finger pointing as in a judgment by Jehovah, he began reciting with unnatural quietness ever crescendoing as to the urgings of a symphony orchestra conductor, ever louder with each line, until at the last word his voice boomed with such thunder the entire space ship shook—

"Mare senza pescha!
Bosco senza lana!
L'uomo senza honore!
Don-na sen-za pu-dor-re!"

Don-na sen-za pu-dor-re reverberated with the deepest and most bodeful profundo I had ever heard. I saw Johannis Miltonis look up with admiration from his scowling silence. The key phrases echoed and reechoed, ringing against the sides of the gym, making the door rattle.

L'uomo senza honore!...Don-na sen-za pu-dor-re! resounded plagently in the corridor and in the distant control room.

L'uomo senza honore!...Don-na sen-za pu-dor-re! suddenly thin and frayed in the distance.

Looking to Marco briefly over one frail shoulder, Little Emily said in a small but clear voice, "That's Dante Allighieri too—the political and angry Dante Allighieri! He is saying, The world has come to such a state as to be like

"Sea without fish!
Forest without trees!
Man without honor!
And woman without modesty!"

Turning back to Wolf, she smiled beatifically into his eyes, he smiled ardently into hers.

Marco made gesture of the fingernail of his right thumb clicking off his teeth. Then, unlike Bartleby, deciding to make the most of what was left to him, he turned from the volleyball court. He would make his talents available to Ma'am, to Stretch, and to Satchmo as umpire of their basketball game. But he would umpire not just the basketball game. No. He would umpire the entire gymnasium floor—the volleyball game, the pool game, Al Ein's continuing efforts at the yo-yo while Ike smiled on with benign wonder, and Mikey Angel's efforts at black, clay and paints into an ever-soaring cathedral of most extraordinary structure splashed with a riot of colors (a construct most unique among God's houses).

More than that, Marco took upon himself the judging of Johannis Miltonis' dour judgments. After making a decision on the basketball court, at the volleyball net, or at the pool table, he pointed a finger at the round-headed Puritan poet and cautioned, "No spik—any-thing!" And then, with an afterthought, he put his finger to his lips and cocked his head, "Please," voice quiet and face smiling gently. For Marco Millionem had finally found an occupation in that room worthy of his emerging ambassadorial talents as the future emissary of the Great Kublai Khan.

As I contemplated Marco's new-found vocation, abruptly the mood in the gaming room seemed to change. I turned—Bartleby was hurrying across the room for the door. Without a second thought I followed after him.

Reaching his side, I paused with him at the door—the jambs shook greatly. When Bartleby opened the door, we felt accosted by a hollow reverberation down the lengths of the corridor. Bartleby beginning to run, I took after him. We plunged for the control room in a dead heat.

Within the control room, a voice sounded like berserk machinery. The crewmen were lined up before the Interspace Com screen, taut with attention.

Captain Goodnik was bent double toward the screen as though bowing.

* * * * * * * * * * * * * * *

"This is the Premier of the United Forces of the West!" The first words I heard as I followed on Bartleby's heels from the outer chamber. Coming over the Interspace Com, Planet Earth Hookup, the voice held the crewmen and Captain Goodnik at attention lined up before the View Screen. "The Commander-In-Chief of the Land and Sea Police, and the Marines and Interplanetray Space Project X." Whatever doubts I had as to the identity of the voice vanished with the last phrase. I didn't have to view the face on the screen— As the size and import of the Titan X venture had become more apparent, so had the Premier's definitions of his responsibilities and, most importantly, of his personal powers. Now, as his voice bore down hard on the final phrase, "and Interplanetary Space Project X," the Interspace Com burped and crackled with static as loud as gun-fire.

Heading up the marshalled crewmen, Captain Goodnik seemed especially attentive to the voice coming from the Interspace Com, to the giganticized face on the screen. He understood and respected such a commanding voice, such an imperious face.

Bartleby understood the moment instinctively— Striding ahead of me rapidly, he took command of the Interspace Com controls. Engaging the P.A. system, he turned the sound up until the voice filled the space ship. There was some uncertainty still about the cooperation of the commandeered crew in our desperate plan and Captain Goodnik's dubeity was a matter of continuing concern. The captain's resistance had been put to sleep, not overcome by Bartleby's repeated warning, "Our last and only hope!"

Now Bartleby's opportunity to demonstrate the urgency of our mission had come.

"This, or—" Instead of finishing the statement, he turned the P.A. system up to its limits. The Premier's voice jumped at us. The *force* of the voice, the magnitude of the stated command levelling all of us, not a single member of the space crew dared move. Only Bartleby seemed up to confronting the overriding presence.

"Now hear this!" The very stilted phrasing. "You hear me, Titan X, hear this!" The betrayal of a sense of desperation in the face of the defiance of his powers made the voice as palpable in its hard reality as, moments before, my bumping against the sides of the spaceship had been in the midst of our levitations in outer space.

As I listened to the voice originating more than a hundred thousand miles away on the planet earth, I felt overwhelmed by my sense of the enormity of the act of spiritual, civil, and human violence represented in the man behind the voice. Bartleby and I, at least, understood—we knew. There were times when I felt even The Living Presences were not above judging the person behind the voice for what he showed himself to be. Now we had to convince the wavering members of the space crew and remove every doubt from Captain Goodnik's mind that if it had not been for the person behind that voice, earth would not be hurtling deeper and deeper into technological warfare and that Bartleby's unvoiced but understood plan was the only alternative.

Otherwise—

It had been said often enough and had long been silently understood. The new moment was not the time to say it again. The voice and face on the Interspace Com were reminders enough, Bartleby knew that and so turned the amplifiers up to their fullest. Premier of the United Forces of the West and Commander-In-Chief of the Land and Sea Police, the Marines and of Interplanetary Space Project X, indeed. The outbreak of Technological warfare had made a reality of what he had always assumed from the moment he had become Premier, what the sensitive among us, such as Bartleby and myself, had begun to understand to be his true nature as soon as we observed his response to initiation of the Space Project X Program earlier in the year.

"You hear me Titan X?— Now hear this!" The reversal of expressions carrying extraordinary force in the moment, I looked at Bartleby quickly. He managed to turn the knob of the P.A. system a decibel more. The voice seemed its own argument against itself. Bartleby knew we had little to fear so long as the voice persisted in speaking for its own thoughts, desires, and judgments.

"The act you have committed is one of Grand Treason against the Covenant of the United Forces of the West and against—" The flicker of an almost inane smile on my lips, I turned only to see its echo on Bartleby's lips. The faces of the crew members froze even more and Captain Goodnik seemed all the more attentive to the Brobdingnagian image on the screen. I turned for relief to the Living Presences. Their faces shared an expression of great curiosity to understand what new arrogance of statement and act the man they had come to associate with the voice was about to produce. Even those like Marco, Mikey Angel, Ike, and Wolf, who carried memories of what an absolute monarch and an emperor was capable, seemed surprised by the dimensions of the Premier's capacity for power. In his turn, each had been known to observe at some time or other in the past few weeks a version of Marco's recent remark, "This ruler of yours, why is it he is not called by the designation which truly characterizes his role—*King* or *Imperial Highness?*" Each time, I had replied as I answered Marco, "But the Covenant of the United Forces of the West does not call for a *king* or *emperor*, only for a *premier* and a bi-cameral legislature, a supreme judicial body, and, as the Covenant itself puts it, 'We, the elective people of the United Forces.'"

"—the office of the Premiership—" as the voice on the Interspace Com boomed, I felt the smile on my lips flutter, "And my august presence!" And there it was, finally said!

I laughed splosively and had to steady myself against the panel of the Interspace Com as I did.

But I was the only one who laughed. Even Bartleby and the Living Presences now faced the screen with rigid seriousness— I saw this as the obverse side of the laughter that shook me, however, for only the crew members and Captain Goodnik seemed genuinely impressed enough to feel the respect the voice and face insisted was due the presence they represented.

"I want to make every effort to persuade you to turn Titan X about and return to its launching site before you become irretrievably involved in whatever ill-advised and irrational scheme you have in mind—" It was this, the adjective he had chosen with which to designate the action we were taking, that again made the entire complex which he represented emergent. *Ill-advised* and *irrational*, indeed. With *his* use of the words so often applied to his own actions, I again had a sense of the climate of culture, society, and government—of human tolerance of the intolerable in public behavior—that had led to his successful preempting of such great powers in the office to which we had elected him.

What we were about was not so easily designated as "ill-advised." The term was too mild a one for what we had in mind. "Desperately-planned," yes, and even "planned from a sense of despair as to what else to do," yes, too. But, "ill-advised—"

As for "irrational," here again much too mild a phrase. This was the rhetoric of deceit that hid, even from itself, the true nature of the crisis facing all of us. We had all come to that. At least, our society had.

Actually, in the face of the question of human survival which was the context of our act, we were acting rationally, all right. We were acting with the same kind of extreme rationality practiced hitherto only by the ancient martyrs, saints, and holiest of divines in their endless quest for what might best redeem and, thus, save mankind.

Bartleby considered our act of desperation to be an attempt at redemption. I was convinced our act could be characterized as "irrational" only in comparison with an even greater irrationality that could be nothing less than insanity.

The question now was, what effect would the voice coming over the Interspace Com have on the crew's wavering belief and the captain's continuing dubeity?

"If you show proper contrition, come to your senses and bring Titan X back *now*—not in five minutes or even after sixty seconds, but right this instant as you hear me reason with you in a most concerned and understanding manner as is fitting of one of my office and person, then I will make every effort to see that the military courts of these United Forces of the West deal with you with leniency—and if they do not, then I shall exercise what powers have been invested in me by the Covenant to see that the lightest sentence possible is imposed upon you. I cannot promise to have you let off with no punishment, for the magnitude of the treasonous act in which you have launched yourself would not permit that. But I can promise you this, I shall do all within my duely-designated powers as Premier of the United Forces of the West to see you are not meted out the ultimate sentence of death, which is the consequences of acts such as yours—"

Bartleby managed to give the amplifier knob another turn.

"Show contrition and turn about in the path on which you have set yourself and all humankind, B-brat!" The P.A. system exploded with a click. Bartleby had turned it off, leaving only the shadow of the voice echoing and reverberating in the spaceship and against its walls, "humankind—humankind-human-kind." But right after it too, harshly, "Brat!— Brat!—Brat!"

It was for humankind we had launched ourselves on the plan we held close and silently among ourselves, even if led by a—*brat*, as the Premier had pronounced the name and intended it to be heard. We knew the way was the last remaining and only way possible. How else might we forestall what we all knew to be impending? What other salvation might there be for planet earth as it hurtled toward the rapids of technological warfare? What?

Suddenly I felt the extreme urgency of time! And I knew Bartleby did too, for right at that moment he turned the knob on the control panel which put the spaceship into motion for a moon-landing.

* * * * * * * * * * * * * * *

You've read a lot in mags and in books and seen a lot on T-V, too, about what it is like to be on the moon. But until you've had the experience yourself, you can never know what it really feels like.

Our walk in space seemed like a flying dream out of my boyhood, yes. Walking on the surface of the moon, then, was like soaring half in a dream and standing half out. Whenever we tried to move was like we were attached to gas-filled balloons. A movement too sudden or a step too large meant risking a fall to the moon's surface in a grotesque posture or, at the least, up-ending. Our jet brakes had to be handled with utmost deftness, even delicacy. Otherwise, our movements became skittish.

That was it, we were like adolescent cats sometimes get. Moving this way and that, forwards, back, sideways and obliquely, if we stopped we found ourselves as though jumping. If we jumped, we leaped as in an athletic contest. And, should anyone of us think of actually leaping, I'm sure he would have soared high above the ridges and hills—only to come crashing to the moon's surface as though dropped from the top of the empire-state building.

Even the slightest miscalculation of movements could mean a bad fall. Bruises were common and fractured arms and legs were always threats.

Bartleby and the space crew had been trained for this aspect of interspace travel, but the training had been for Titan satellite of Saturn not the earth's moon. Bartleby and Captain Goodnik had to recalculate for the moon landing.

The principle involved had to do with the effects of mass and distance interacting upon each other under the influence of various solar gravitational fields created by the interaction among all the planets and their moons upon each other and they, individually and together, on the sun. Specifically, Bartleby and the captain refigured the moon's and earth's masses relative to their distance from each other and to the sun's mass and distance. These figures were compared with their previous calculations of similar factors related to Saturn and its Titan satellite. Adjustments were thus made and a formula for walking on the moon's surface was worked out. Had we not been in charge of a commandeered project, we could have easily called back to planet earth and received detailed calculations used on previous moon-landings. As it was, we had to improvise.

Even at that, those who wished to take a moonwalk had to play the situation by ear, or rather, more accurately, by breath. The Living Presences and I (all eager to make the second venture outside the space ship) had to relearn not only how to step and move, but also how to breathe. The very force of a breath too quick or too big might be enough to up-end us, so Bartleby told us.

And so we soon discovered.

We might have been children again, moving about and tumbling in invisible snow with an undersurface of ice—so studied was our movements and so precarious, our footing. But we braved it and we managed it, the Living Presences, Bartleby, and I. In spite of the treacherous footing, in spite of our frequent tumbles, our multiple lacerations and bruises, I, for one, would not have missed that walk, not for anything. For those brief moments of walking about on the surface of the moon might have been the very last moments we would ever again spend outside the space ship or anywhere else for that matter. They might have been the last moments there would be any surface of the moon for anyone anytime ever again to be walked on, to attempt flights to or even to look at longingly from the planet earth. They might have been the last moments for such walking on, flying to, or looking longingly at for any and all other bodies in the solar system and the universe, and beyond—for that matter.

If—

If—

If—

But, for now we were out and stepping about on the eerie—now too hot, now suddenly (with a few steps) too cold—now too dark and now too luminescent—stone-frozen surface covered with something that seemed like moon-dust—

Into which we often sank (sometimes knee-deep), Bartleby, the L.P.'s and I.

As for the labrador retriever, it seemed to be in its element—loping boundlessly.

We might have been in a fun house on an invisible Coney Island. Then, again, we might have been on a gigantic ballroom floor of ancient antiquity, minuetting, zardoshing, and polkaing with each other. Emily and Wolf seemed to be minuetting and zardoshing, that is—with Bartleby Bratt occasionally cutting in on Wolf and trying to dance Emily away, but only momentarily. Yet persistently and frequently. For no sooner were Wolf and Emily returned to each other's arms and dancing smoothly in great legato sweeps of moon movements, than Bartleby again cut in. It was as though he felt he had the right to romantic rivalry and participation. I decided he had come to feel like one of them.

With the revelation, I saw him with new eyes, almost.

In the meantime, Ma'am and Satchmo might as well have been polkaing with Stretch making it a sashaying threesome as they moved in sudden glissandoes alternating with syncopated steppings, hopping, and jumpings to the riffing of Satchmo's cornet and Stretch's basso hummings.

When Bartleby was content to accept a third part in place of the rare half partnership with Emily, Emily, Wolf, and my young genius friend actually touched gloved hands to the accompaniment of the petite poetess' new improvised verse—

"We now walk upon the moon's face—
Out of space—
Out of time.

We will dance at God's pace—
From now 'til e-ter-ni-ty-y-y!"

Wolf's duetting rococo scatting dropped off into a coughing (scattering the new threesome this way and that way in crazy-cat movements of jig-saw leaps and slides). His gloved hands separating from Emily's and Bartleby's, Wolf scittered across the moon's surface alone like a great fish fighting an invisible line running out from his two former partners. Finally, braking his movements with his jets, he returned striding, striding like an adolescent sheep dog controlled by, not controlling his movements, as he was brought by this way and that as on an invisible leash.

I experienced panic for the slight composer, both during his fugue away from his partners in the threesome and also on his return in great ever-meandering baroque loping strides, this way, that way—all the way around, until finally back. But my fears were unfounded. For, as facile as his humming and scatting were (the latter an entirely new but quickly mastered musical mode for the rococo Austrian composer), so his sense of balance. Wolf recovered his footing with a brisk rhythm enabling him to return to Emily's side and raise his gloved hand to hers. As he did, accidentally he brushed against Bartleby, whose turn now it was to go hurtling away—but head-over-heels, tumbling as it were, until finally, sliding to a stop (as though at home plate) rose to his feet and strode slowly and surely in the greatest giant steps imaginable all the way back. Returned finally, he too raised his right gloved hand to Emily's left even as Wolf had raised his left gloved hand to Emily's right, moments before— And the three were again engaged.

Emily undertaking still another verse, the three attempted a minuette *ă trois*. The view they presented was like nothing so much as that of three exotic mating birds. Watching them, I had a sense that for the first time since her resurrection by the Time Machine Emily could indeed be spoken of in her own words as "inebriate of air," and "debauchée of dew," the moon's lack of "air" combining with its attenuated pull to create the conditions for this to be possible—a veritable "lunacy" being not only hers but also Wolf's and Bartleby's.

As for Satchmo, Ma'am, and Stretch, the walk that turned out to be their dance on the moon was something else. The effects showed initially in Satchmo, for his voice was not just silvery and nimble (as cornet's are wont to be) but also sounded more and more like a full-throated trumpet of most extraordinary size and voice—now in the highest of high registers and now in the deepest basso profundo, syncopated too. I had a thought, *Satchmo must find a way of building a musical instrument which, under the normal conditions of earth, permit the playing of such a range of notes at will.*

As Satchmo played to their trio dancing, Stretch's basso profundo humming provided rhythm not unlike that of a base fiddle as Satchmo and Ma'am moved about the pole of his steady and stationary sashaying. Every now and again, the three of them to go polkaing and waltzing through the whorling moon-dust left everywhere by the movements of Wolf, Emily, and Bartleby.

Suddenly, Marco from out of nowhere— First to Wolf, Emily, and Bartleby, in an attempt to make their trio a quartet. But they having difficulties of their own as a threesome, he did an aboutface and went scurrying through a tornado of moon-dust to impose his urges on Satchmo, Ma'am, and Stretch. As Ma'am made grand and slow gestures as though conducting Satchmo and Stretch in their dance with her in a music of their own making, momentarily Marco found enough room to add his presence. Momentarily the second trio seemed on its way to becoming a quartet. His robust movements impacting their syncopated rhythms—now against theirs, now with theirs—the four surged in a most marvelously syncopated counterpoint. The cornet and basso profundo humming crescendoed and crescendoed until all else, Wolf's small voice or rococo scatting and Emily's even smaller saying of still another of her improvised verses, was drowned out. My eardrums fluttering as though about to burst, I knew the remainder of the Living Presences were affected too for they seemed to go scattering wildly, this way and that, as on a beserk roller coaster, twisting and turning, rising, and then suddenly falling—almost loop the loop.

I snapped off my intercom.

I knew when the others had turned off their intercoms, for suddenly whatever of their faces I could see through the visors seemed greatly relaxed and, like mine, their movements on the moon's surface were again under the control of their own efforts by foot and, when soaring, by jets. But for Satchmo, Ma'am and Stretch.

As for them, they went on and on—polka, into waltz, into zardosh. At the same time, Ma'am's conducting became more rhythmical, and broader too. Moving closer and closer to Satchmo, until the visor's of their helmets touched, she let herself be turned and twisted by Satchmo's free hand around Stretch (the three of them moving to sounds only they could hear)—

Until, Ma'am's arms collapsed to her sides, and the three dancers fell fast against each other.

I felt I should have turned my head away quickly from the view, as though suddenly the curtain had gone rattling up on a window in a private house.

But as easily and as instantly as they had come together, the three parted. And when they did, they put their gloved hands up to each other (one of Ma'am's to one of Stretch's and the other one to Satchmo's, the two men, in turn, putting their free hands up to each other). The palms of their hands touching *á trois*, they now moved in the slowest and easiest rhythms imaginable.

Suddenly Marco leaped at random, this way and that—now toward the first and unsuccessful trio of Wolf-Emily-Bartleby rapidly on its way to becoming a duet between Wolf and Emily, alone, and now toward the successful trio on its way to fulfillment as a *ménage á trois*. Only to end up in a limbo solo.

Marco's leaps setting it off, the labrador retriever rebounded with such abandon, up—up—up, until, it finally sailing down a thousand yards away from us, we thought it had jumped so high it went right over the moon into outer space.

Reassured by the return of the dog, I snapped my Intercom back on— The silver tones of the cornet sounded like a great organ playing the Anniversary Waltz. At the same time, the other intercoms turned on too, Emily's voice came small and sweet again—

"Oh, here we are
On the day we are born,
Singing our birthdays
On the day we are to—"

Swinging into a great harmonious humming, marked by the intervals of the returned labrador retriever's barks, the chorus of voices drowned out Emily's last word, a word that might become the L.P.'s last during the duration of their Time Machine resurrection. Everyone joined in, including Ike, Ali Ein, the Mahoot, Marty, Mikey Angel, and the labrador retriever.

As the L.P.'s sang thus and so (the labrador retriever's bark proving a unique background), Bartleby and I hopped, skipped, and gently jumped back to the space ship door, through which we were immediately admitted. Behind us, the L.P.'s were left to cavort in universal harmony, with the labrador retriever bounding about freely as though inspired by the magic of celestial bounce.

* * * * * * * * * * * * * * *

The face on the main screen was unmistakable, even though taut, deeply shadowed, and hollow. Conflicting emotions leaving him in a state of collapse, Captain Goodnik yielded his place at the control panel to Bartleby. Quickly, Bartleby pulled the face on the screen into sharp definition. The Premier was sitting in the Technological Control Room of the United Forces of the West, alone. He was facing multiple T.V. views of the far-flung battlefronts, on the ground and in the air. Every now and again, he turned fullfaced to the camera connecting him with Titan X. He didn't have to say a word—the multiple T-V views of rapidly advancing technological warfare spoke for themselves. The

Iron Fist had closed tighter and tighter, squeezing the globe to bursting.

How much more could the planet take before exploding?

Captain Goodnik collapsed, the Titan X crew echoed the face on the main screen a half hundred times over. Disembodied and mechanical in responses, the crew reminded me of the tin soldiers I had watched Bartleby marshall on the floor of his office the afternoon of my decision to substitute Project Living Presences for Project Transformation of Genius.

I thought of the L.P.'s now afloat on the crest of sublime bliss as they giant-stepped across the moon's surface with the labrador retriever bounding hither and yon all around them. As I thought of them, it was as though I were contemplating a reversal. During the past months, the L.P.'s had seemed to emerge with each new terrestrial involvement they shared with Bartleby and me. A subtle change seemed to come over them. I could not say exactly what it was, but as I thought of them at that moment they seemed no longer as ethereal and otherworldly as they had when first resurrected. Even their eerie seven league boots gambolings on the lunar surface enhanced this impression for they seemed to enjoy a sense of the new elasticity of their physical movements. With each passing month, they had shown more care in moving about. On the moon's surface, they moved with such care—even as they soared and even flew a little(as flying fishes sometimes flew)—it was as though the bodies they inhabited were all they had ever known and would ever know. I had seen dancers and athletes treat their bodies with such respect, rarely ordinary humans— I had not expected resurrected spirits to show so much care for such temporal trappings. Gradually I became aware of their faces and bodies as such— As the months went on, I noticed how foreshortened Emily's chin was, that Stretch had a wart over his right eyebrow, on his right cheek, and on his chin, that Ike's face was pitted with small pox scars, and that Marco looked like a football quarterback with the widest shoulders ever. With each passing month, their flesh seemed to become more solid and heavy on their frames. But more than that, I had come to sense their individual personalities, their distinct characters until, just a few minutes earlier as I had last seen them on the surface of the moon, most of them had seemed animated with a subtle warmth as though they interacted with each other as more than spirits— as flesh and emotions now, even with passion (as they had, indeed, in the gaming room).

Even the frailest of them, Emily and Wolf, seemed more like humans now than did the crew of Titan X, standing frozen at the central Interspace Com Screen. Most curiously, I did not find it so extraordinary that the L.P.'s seemed so. For during the ordeal of the crew's incipient revolt of some hours earlier, the L.P.'s seemed to have emerged with Bartleby's triumph over Captain Goodnik's protest. The subtle transsubstantiation of the past several months had accelerated greatly during the lunar journey (the farther we travelled into the heavens, the more substantial the L.P.'s seemed to become as living presences). They became as involved in the outcome of Bartleby's oratorical struggle for the rebels' souls as I— When Bartleby's good sense and fine rhetoric triumphed, I sensed as much emotional relief in the L.P.'s as I experienced myself. But more than that, in the space walk, in the gaming room, then on the lunar surface, they had become so entangled with each other in interrelationships (especially through the two romantic triangles, one shaping up firmly and the other falling away into a one-to-one romance) they were put in connection with levels of existence few of them had known even during their legitimate lifetimes on the planet earth. Certainly Emily experienced with Wolf something she had hitherto known only as imagination and poetry, and Stretch, Ma'am and Satchmo had together a depth of personal involvement they had known before only in their work. As for Ike, Ali Ein, the Mahoot, Marty, and Mikey Angel—well, they had come to know each other as persons on an hour-to-hour basis, not as charismatic life forces. Marco, of course, was something entirely else. But in trying so desperately to live up to his biography, he became, in some ways, the most humanized of the L.P.'s, the most usefully humanized.

The above was demonstrated most at the moment of confrontation with the Premier. Right then, we missed the L.P.'s in the control room, missed their presence greatly. Realizing what a difference their absence made, I became convinced that something of a reversal had taken place between Bartleby, Captain Goodnik and the International Crew, on the one hand, and the L.P.'s on the other. More than that, this reversal put an even greater distance between the two groups—which seemed curious to me, until I understood human nature made this so whenever such reversals took place. More than that, I found myself serving as the last link remaining between the two groups. At the same time, I felt closer in responses to the L.P.'s than I did to Captain Goodnik and the International Crew, perhaps even closer to the L.P.'s than to Bartleby too now. This was why I missed the L.P.'s so at the moment of confrontation.

I must admit this, I also resented them some. For while we, within, were at the moment of crucial confrontation—with the face on the main screen, with ourselves, and with the earth's and solar system's destiny—the L.P.'s, on the other hand, were having the time of their present or any other life. This, perhaps, defined the reversal most—while mere mortals were forced to grapple with the question of all our destinies, the immortals were having a good time on the moon's surface in a manner most terrestrial and human.

What defined the reversal even more was that even as I missed the L.P.'s, I had a sense of extraordinary communication with them leaping like inebriated wolves on the moon's surface. I experienced something like knowledge of a sudden pause in their cavortings, followed by a sense of their having turned together to face Titan X as though tuning in an aura of portentous disquiet emanating from within.

And I knew! I knew!—

As the door from the Gravitation-equallizer Room opened, I gasped with relief as the L.P.'s filed in, climbed out of their moon garbs, and gathered around me. Now I could face up to the moment confronting all of us.

My sense of rescue was so great, I did not notice the labrador retriever was not among them.

As for Bartleby, he was so busy manipulating the dials on the control panel, he seemed to continue oblivious even of the L.P.'s presence. He continued so even after having a second face on a neighboring screen.

The second face was puffed and googly-eyed with shock, yet I recognized the recently elevated Chairman of the United Forces of the East. As the formerly bland, now bloated features of the Chairman were pulled in clearly, I wondered what Bartleby had in mind. In seconds, the two earth tyrants would be facing each other and hearing each other through our screens. Such a confrontation between the two men had not been possible through any facilities whatsoever on the planet they divided between themselves.

Was Bartleby going to try to get the two strong men to communicate with each other, to speak and to listen to each other?

But how could he?— They refused to communicate with him even!

Still Bartleby manipulated dials.

Immediately after the Chairman's face, Bartleby brought in a multitude of views of blazing terrestrial warfronts. Central to these, grossly grisly views of each Bloc's forest of atomic and hydrogen missiles sprouted, waiting, waiting. The buttons were at the Premier's and the Chairman's fingertips. Bartleby's work at the dials was clearly defined and dramatic.

Yet, the two titans seemed as passive in their responses to the confrontation as two mechanical creatures. Remembering the International Crew's similar response to the confrontation with the Premier's face fifteen minutes earlier, I had a sense of panic so overwhelming all responses were erased. Like intricate and delicate machinery(programmed to perform with the greatest efficiency, and instantaneously, when the correct message had been received) in the face of new and unexpected situations they seemed to cease functioning.

With the realization, I found myself disproportionately concerned about Emily and Ma'am, how the tensions of the moment might affect their delicate responses. Curiosily, I even became worried about Wolf's person. At the same time, I felt a reassurance that Stretch, Marty, Ike, the Mahoot, Ali Ein and Mikey Angel were present. I found myself grinning idiotically to the thought that, sometime during the moment, Johannis Miltonnis was bound to unloose one of his jeremiads of most doomful sound.

I sensed all of them as never before, a source of substantial support, not merely as abstractions. They were with us all the way, in the fullest way possible. For while the moment froze the rest of us, the L.P.'s seemed to come even more alive. They could not have been any more so had they been real nerves, flesh and blood.

"Your Excellency, Sir!" Bartleby addressed the face on the central screen. Deep and resonant, his voice sounded as before his transformation. I understood—his recent successful struggle with Captain Goodnik and the rebelling spacecrew had been as decisive for him as it had been for the L.P.'s. Where they had become fully engaged in our condition by the persuasive force of Bartleby's rhetoric and the magnitude of his mission, Bartleby himself had come out as a triumphant and, therefore, powerful individual who was just beginning to understand the dimensions of his personal force. In short, they had become a deeply involved and concerned "we," whereas he had emerged as a vibrant leader—I.

I knew this for hadn't I seen what I had seen in the gaming room less than a half hour earlier?

And now, as Bartleby's voice boomed, I watched the Premier's head turn quickly from the multitude of battle scenes and hydrogen missile sights he viewed on the multiple T-V screens of the Control Panel for the United Forces of the West.

"Lt. Bartleby!" The Premier's voice rasped as he refocussed his attention.

"Respectfully requesting your Excellency's imemediate audience, Sir—"

"Lt.—" the Premier's voice soared precipitously. "I have given you my last command— The matter had been turned over to the martial courts!"

"But, your Serene Excellency, if you would grant me this one moment—"

"You are interrupting a most fateful moment, Lt.— You hear?"

"I hear, Sir!" Bartleby's voice seemed to deepen even more. "It's about this—moment, that I presume to make communication with you—" A conciliatory tone.

Expectation flickering in the shell of the Premier's face, he seemed to bend all the closer to the sending camera, then to the screen, turning it up, tuning in Bartleby full, "You've come to your sense, Lt.— The Titan Cobalt Warhead, you want to know where to aim it on the control beam?"

"Your Serenity—" Bartleby's voice worked under excruciating control now.

"Your return to sanity is none too soon, Lt!" The Premier's voice shook the space ship control room. "You see on your intercom., don't you, the Chairman of the Opposing Forces, his finger poised at the button that will send his atomic missiles flying?— I, of course, have no other choice but to stand just as ready!— The moment his finger makes a move, I, of course, have no other alternative—" His arm stretched to the Control Panel of the United Forces of the West and his finger moved to the fateful button, resting tautly.

"I see on the intercom, yes," Bartleby's deeply modulated voice moved carefully, "both of you!— And both of you see each other on your intercoms!— And now you can hear each other too!" Bartleby spun several knobs until the Chairman's voice sounded from the second screen as boomfully and bodefully as did the Premier's on the central screen. "But most importantly, both of you can see and hear me too!" Bartleby's voice overrode both the Premier's and the Chairman's like a deafening explosion. He strode greatly from one screen to the other. "See me!— Hear me!"

As Bartleby bellowed, I was so startled I looked away from the screen to his face. His face looked like that of a human juggernaut. Yet it showed something much more. I looked to the L.P.'s for help in understanding Bartleby's emotion. None of them seemed troubled, not even Wolf or Emily.

Yet there was the evidence of my own ears and eyes. Bartleby had set up a special confrontation among the three men in command, not between the Premier and the Chairman and the rest of us. Bartleby's wording was unmistakable for he had said, "me," not *us*. He had said, "Both of you can see and hear me too!" And right after, the command, "See me!—Hear me!"

With the realization, I trembled. For the awesome moment seemed to have become one among three giant individuals, rather than three forces representing three different ways people viewed the world.

I, at least, saw the moment as such.

As for the L.P.'s they seemed attentive to the moment but, as yet, not worried—not really worried. The crewmen and Captain Goodnik seemed to freeze all the more for they seemed absolutely dumfounded. Yet even they did not seem to share the indefinable extra uneasiness I felt.

I became all the more fearful.

Johannis Miltonis watched Bartleby with growing interest. A few hours earlier her had shown admiration for Bartleby's rhetorical *tour de force* in bringing Captain Goodnik around, but this, now, was something else. Bartleby's new confrontation was of cosmic scope. The youthful Puritan poet and tractarian observed the youthful cosmophysicist as though studying a possible protagonist for an epic poem. He seemed to be experiencing a moment such as would be his main preoccupation both as poet and political pamphleteer to the end of his days.

As for the L.P.'s, they seemed to take the moment as a virtuoso ploy on Bartleby's part. Perhaps this was why Johannis Miltonis had been set on the track of his deepening thoughts. Because I knew Johannis Miltonis so well, I became fearful of the moment. I had read all his works, I had read about his public and private life of dedication to a harsh taskmaster. I became all the more fearful, for Bartleby—for all of us, in that space ship and on the planet earth.

I feared the sound of Johannis Miltonis' voice thrusting through the moment as much as I now trembled to the new sound in Bartleby's voice.

I knew what it might have been like had two Old Testament Prophets appeared on the scene together. What would the one prophet be thinking while the other created an awesome confrontation between himself and creation's two greatest tyrants? And the purpose of that confrontation, to force them into communication and, if communication, then into an alliance with each other as the only way either could save himself from the far-greater threat the boy genius presented himself as being to both of them, what would the first prophet think of that? What was Johannis Miltonis thinking of Bartleby's ploy?

Just then I had a view of the moon's furface. One moment eerily luminescent, the next moment densely dark, the arid and horned surface seemed was broken by the occasional intoxicated leapings of the labrador retriever. Glancing away, for a moment I had a view of another planet which looked like the moon's moon. As I viewed the dark surface of continental shapes as distant as thought and comprehension, I knew I was watching the planet earth. Still, at that moment, the earth, not the moon, looked lunar.

The next moment my thoughts returned to the space ship and the control panels of the Intercom. Again I was held by two gigantic full-length views: Standing at the Control Panels of the United Forces of the West, the Premier extended his right index finger to a single button; the Chairman of the United Forces of the East stretched his left index finger to a single button in his Control Panels. At the same time, Bartleby loomed over the Control Panel of Titan X, both index fingers stretched forth.

The Intercom Viewers flickered. What force of so great a disturbance could possibly be short-circuiting our bathsphere and ionosphere communication waves? Or was the source of the interfence from within the space ship? With the last thought, whimsically I escaped to the possibility that nothing more than a sudden hail of random meteorites or ven, possibly, the labrador retriever's ever crescendoing leaps above the space ship down to the earth and then up and over the space ship again. With the last, I smiled idiotically.

The faces on the screens thrust now, overbig, then dwindled, now small and now distant—cross-hatched. Bartleby cleared the screens quickly.

"And the two of you, you hear?" He shattered the moment of new clarity. "While your fingers stretch threateningly toward hydrogen missile buttons, I present both of you and all humankind a common threat. The moment either of you touches his missile button, I shall press both of mine."

I had guessed right, on all accounts! And I felt nauseous with the thought.

The Premier and the Chairman faced their screens full. How alike their faces seemed, not just in tone but also in shape. In total shock, their eyelids were puffed shells, their eyes were hardly visible and their mouths were shapeless.

"You see," Bartleby pursued relentlessly. "I have one finger at the atomic reactor control for instantaneous start and maximum acceleration—the other finger stretches to the button which would detonate the Cobalt Warhead."

Pausing long enough for his stretched fingers to galvanize their eyes, he plunged ahead, "Your Excellency—Your Chairmanship—do you know what would happen if I pushed both buttons at the same time?" His voice broke, but he managed to continue, "The moon would be turned into a gigantic meteorite—" And shouting wildly, "Sent on a random spin through the solar system—"

"But—" the Premier sputtered, "that would mean throwing the entire earth and moon out of gravitational orbit—"

"Ex-actly!" Bartleby's voice broke again. His face became all the more rigid.

"That would upset the gravitational balance among the solar planets, their satellites, and the sun—" the Chairman now.

"That would mean turning the entire solar system into a cosmic bomb!" The Premier.

"That would mean bursting the solar system wide, followed by a chain reaction in our gallaxy, triggering the setting off of infinite gallaxies behind!" The Chairman again.

"Ex-actly! Ex-actly! Exactly!" Bartleby's voice thundering through the space ship, "Worlds, universes, cosmos, and galaxies without end—" He broke off into a fit of coughing and harsh gasps.

For seconds, I feared for him. But within seconds, he was tall and taut again.

The moment was entirely between Bartleby and the two earth tyrants. Yet, feeling like a hand that had been crushed in a slamming door, I huddled, trembling, against the L.P.'s. I clung to them as though they were now the only possible survivors of what now faced us in our islanded world. For, as though terrorized into vanishing into the private caves of their individual psyches, Captain Goodnik and the spacecrew seemed extinct. Curiously, at that moment, the L.P.'s seemed more of blood and flesh than any human aboard the space ship, for their responses now seemed more like living community organisms. I had a sense about them that they still extended Bartleby belief even in the horrendous moment of the showdown, belief which I no longer had the courage, even though the wish, to give him.

As a boy, I had read about 19th century Czarist officers testing each other's courage in a trial referred to as "Russian Roulette." The moment between Bartleby Bratt and the two earth planet tyrants was like that game, only more—the revolver he held was aimed at all of us, and none of the chambers were empty.

We aboard the spaceship knew this. What we also knew was that Bartleby was bluffing. So the game was one in which Bartleby's bluff must not be called. Otherwise—

The outcome of the moment depended on the Premier and the Chairman not reading Bartleby's bluff correctly. This, in turn, depended on how convincing Bartleby was and how adept the two tyrants were at interpreting both his character and his overriding emotion of the moment.

And all of this depended on the extent to which they had been corrupted, therefore blinded, by their powers.

The situation was so extraordinarily a warped one, for the first time we found ourselves hoping the two leaders of the world's most powerful forces had been so corrupted they retained no traces of humanity but were possessed by an absolute arrogance of personal power. Otherwise, they might see through Bartleby's bluff.

We trembled on the lip of the moment.

Bartleby, however, loomed even more a t the Interspace Communication Panel.

Whose tyranny would win out?—The moral tyranny of the Premier's arrogance and the real tyranny of the Chairman's power, or the bluff tyranny of Bartleby's threat? With the thought, I looked away from Bartleby's distorted face with a sense of strange disquiet. Turning to the main interspace viewer and to the one adjoining, I felt I might have been looking at three masks fashioned exactly the same.

My disquiet becoming panic, I turned to the L.P.'s. But in their faces now, puzzlement, even hurt. I had to look away from them too. Only Captain Goodnik and the crewmembers remained dumb, blank-faced.

The moment was unbearable.

But only for a moment.

The next moment, the Premier's face flickered, then collapsed, "I-I'll have to consult with my advisers and with the Assembly." As he spoke, his face seemed to drain until it seemed flabby, even pulpy.

As though a switch had been thrown, the Chairman's face too, now, collapsed. His voice became concilliatory, "Let me—confer with the Delegates of the Provinces—please."

The last, so breathlessly unexpected a word, sent the two earth planet leaders, almost as one, backing rapidly away from their Control Panels. The two interspace televiewers gaped empty.

His fingers dropping away from the two buttons like broken twigs, Bartleby collapsed into the televiewer's seat. I heard horrendous breath rush from his lungs.

He beginning to tremble, I bent to him.

"Let me alone—" He turned his face away from me.

"Why?—" I wanted him to know how pleased we were with him. We were grateful to him and also proud to have been a part of so momentous a crisis so well carried off.

"I don't deserve—" but he didn't finish. Instead, he looked away from my bewilderment.

"I know now what and why they are what they are—" he finally turned back to me. His eyes then flitting from face to face of the crewmembers, suddenly I had a sense of great lost—I looked about the space ship desperately for the once fey and recently all-too-human faces. But the L.P.'s were nowhere in sight. Every single one of them had vanished, even Johannis Miltonis.

With the realization, I knew what Bartleby was about to say.

"That second—when the Premier hesitated on the precipice of decision—" Bartleby's voice soared through the moment, until it shook, "I experienced what it meant to be on the precipice of a moment—" his voice broke, "to-be-so-caught-up in a mo-ment, whatever followed seemed natural—even in-ev-i-table!" His voice was an alto tremolo, "During that moment, I could-have—pressed the buttons." His face turned away in agony, "Out oa a sheer sense of the overflow of power!" Frayed, his voice vanished.

I had guessed right, why it was the mercurial L.P.'s had vanished.

"To do it ar-bi-tra-ri-ly! Just so—Out of a sheer sense of overflowing power!" Bartleby's voice was hardly audible, yet he had to go on as though to work the act out in words and thus deplete its insistent energy.

"I was sure—I was certain then—the Premier and the Chairman were themselves victims. They had been pushed into the moment by history, science, and the circumstances of power. They were the victims of the vanity of human—wishes—gone astray. They had been put in the process of doing what they were about to do just as inevitably as an apple must sooner or later drop to earth, unless it is picked."

I was left gasping with the last. Right then, more than ever I thought of the vanished L.P.'s, most especially of Ike. Had it been possible, I guessed the L.P.'s might have returned the time dimensions back to the present. Yet, perhaps, the need for them was over, and they must have felt this before they did their disappearing act back into time and history. Or, feeling that Bartleby was lost to them—even if only for a moment—had they felt that all the world was lost to them?

Through my thoughts, suddenly Captain Goodnik's voice, "Yes, but unlike the Premier and the Chairman—" revived from his state of shock the captain was speaking overbig and too quickly, "You, at least, came to your senses without being threatened."

"I didn't!" Bartleby shouted, then his voice soared hoarsely again. "I was so exhausted, I could no more commit the act than I could follow through with the thought—"

Then, a moment later, "And—as Ali Ein might have said—'So you have it, Relativity!'

I was tempted to add, "$E = mc^2$, too!" But decided I wouldn't.

All of us, the spacecrew, Captain Goodnik and I were looking at him now. In my mind's ear, I heard Johannis Miltonis intoning like a darkling deacon, "Of man's first disobedience and the fruit of that immortal tree, I sing! I sing! I sing!" Each of the *sings* resounded like a lamentation. Even in his absence, I became greatly impatient with the world's most eloquent spokesman for elegiac sin, repentance, and redemption. His eloquence in evoking sin and damnation so infinitely greater than when he sang of repentance and redemption must have cast such a pall on the L.P.'s they preferred to be triggered back into time than face the lugubrious tone of the present against which he fulminated.

The spaceship levitating, I was rescued from the thought. We were rising from the moon's surface. Momentarily poised, the next moment we were hurtling straight upward and outward and around as though on the return line of a parabola.

As we swept off on our way back, I looked into the interspace telescope viewer. The mottled surface of the moon's moon grew rapidly larger straight ahead—until, suddenly, the markings were unmistakable as continental masses, surging mountain ranges and winding rivers.

The world! The earth. We were on our return journey home.

Scatting rococo hemidemisemiquavers of an extraordinarily lively Mozart chamber piece, Bartleby worked himself around to a poem I recognized as one of Little Emily's. This followed by another I knew to be a Johannis Miltonis poem which, in turn, was followed by one sounding like Little Emily translating Marco's recitation of Dante Allighieri, Bartleby finally worked his way through to one of his own. A moment later, I had a sense—he was improvising. But unlike the poetry he last composed before he entered *Project Transformation of Genius*, the lines he now recited showed themselves to have been amalgamated through a variety of influences transmuted into his own. The lines were as delicate as Little Emily's, as ora-supulchral as Johannis Miltonis', and as darkly lyrical as Dante Allighieri's. At the same time, what made them his own, they were both scientifically and socially perceptive. Bartleby's voice, Bartleby's vision, Bartleby's poetry.

Delighted with the return and full maturing of Bartleby's finest talents thought to be sacrificed months before, I looked over my shoulder to express my pleasure to the crew. What I saw made the moment sheer joy—Such a drib-a-drib-dribbling and a pas-a-pass-passing of Stretch's basketball and a pock-a-pock-pocking of Emily's and Wolf's volleyball as I have never seen before, even in the miniature gaming room. At the same time, the crew members stood shoulder to shoulder at the observation room, as the spaceship followed its line of flight home. Moving among them, Captain Goodnik and Bartleby Bratt spread cheer, person to person.

Together, we leaned forward to the observation window. Directly ahead, the globe of the earth. As Titan X carried us hurtling forward, the globe seemed to come directly at us out of the wrong end of a telescope. Until, as though the telescope had been turned around, suddenly what was miniature and out of reach now seemed overlarge and but fingertips away.

And there it was again, the Planet Earth, the sole known habitat of the special cosmic manifestation known as, *human* life, secretly and silently pulling us back to where we belonged.

"You see?" Bartleby said with a wise smile. "As Ike would put it, 'the force of gravity.' "

My eyes on the sunrise, I had a view of land masses, great bodies of water, mountain ranges and rivers rising toward us. In the background, sounds of the dribbling basketball and the pocking volleyball. At my side, Bartleby composed still another of his poems, both lyrical and legato, counterpointed by Ma'am's deep contralto rendition of Mahler's "The Song Of The Earth."

Right then, for the briefest instant on the Interspace Con Viewer I saw a flickering mass of shades looking very much like the essences of the L.P.'s, rejoined by the labrador retriever. One of them—it might have been Little Emily or was it Johannis Miltonis?—even waved to us. I watched a mouth move in what might have been a "So long!" A moment later—was it possible?—the mouth shaped the words, "*Paradise Regained*!—Regained! Regained!" The words echoed through the heavens.

A moment later, the figures and words faded, leaving behind only the labrador retriever. Half emerged against the multiple stars, he looked ambitious to become one of the constellations. I thought how fine it might be if all the L.P.'s joined hands and formed a single great configuration to overlook the earth planet from the heavens for all time eternal, the monitors and guardians of all us mortals. What better monument could there be to the day we had just completed?

The next moment, the spaceship was braking greatly and turning about. Then, lowering, lowering in a sweep forward, aft, and down, we hovered. Through the clouds, a sudden view of a flock of seagulls. Directly below us, a multitude of peaceniks waiting to welcome us with a millionfold open arms.

And I knew we were home.

ALLHALLOWSMAS
(A dramatic opera in III STAGES)

ALLHALLOWSMAS

Author's Curtain Word

The audience has a view of two enclosures, an outer stage (larger), and an inner stage (smaller). The inner stage bustles with a colorful variety of humanity of all ages and hues. Costumes are most extravagant and gay, as are gestures and movements. Some carry hand masks and some, floor masks (that is, masks on poles).

Closest to the audience (front stage), the outer stage presents a living room, furnished as a fiftyish woman of certain refined tastes might furnish it. The room seems dedicated to the art of quiet loitering in easy chairs and sofas. T-V sets fill the room with multiple images and multiple sounds (giving the effects of a Picasso painting). The viewer has a peculiar sense of two worlds going at the same time in exactly the same place on two entirely different planes of living (two entirely different dimensions of time, tone, and actuality). As the action progresses, these two worlds do not resolve themselves but produce a third, one superimposed on the others. As a result, characters in the play often seem stretched on a wrack.

In the background, as the curtain rises, sounds of a Halloween horn and the view of a jack-o-lantern on a pole.

In the first few minutes, nothing but T-V sets, flashing and sounding big. A screen here flutters with ribbons, another shows snow, still another flutters a picture on and off, still another switches channels. Likewise, the sound goes high, goes low, goes off, then goes on. Not a soul visible on stage, the T-V sets seem to operate with a will of their own.

Some of the screens flash with space shows, journeys into the cosmos shows, and futuristic shows.

The flashing and booming, rising and then diminishing, give the illusion of a sterile fireworks, sputting and puffing, of a multiple bower of refrigerated rainbows, bleached snow and unfertile rain, a rain that would parch, rather than quench the earth's thirst.

The stage is empty of humans for extended minutes. Until, when it seems the play is to be nothing but the fragmented, futuristic present, human beings appear finally.

First, a solitary woman, alone, in slippers and a sort of lounging robe. She saunters investigatively onto the scene, then sidles, twists, and turns, giving her side to the audience, then giving the audience her backside, finally turning full front to the audience. The lights go up slowly and then she is spotlighted.

The woman, hesitant, searching — "Jimmie?" She looks into the audience, about the stage, into the left and right wing. "Jimmie?" (A little louder). She runs to one wing, then the other, and finally flings out to the audience, but not too loudly, "Jimmie, Jimmie, Janet and Will. Where are you all?"

Voices from off stage, one (distantly), then another (less distantly), still another and another (until the voices, male and female, sound near stage from backstage), "Cloe! Cloe! Cloe! Where are you?"

The woman, with delight, "Right here where I'm supposed to be, where else?"

One by one and in groups of twos and threes, the men and women come on stage, giggling, laughing, and bustling—from both wings. When they're all on, the lights go down abruptly, leaving only the woman spotlighted, the others erased in dim lights.

"There you are, Cloe!" One, then another.

"We looked everywhere for you." In chorus.

"There I am?" The woman.

"Of course, there you are!" In chorus.

"I repeat, there I am?" The woman.

"Yes, Cloe, there you are."

"But you knew all along where I was."

"We knew all along where you were?" In chorus.

"Yes, you knew."

"How would we know?" In chorus.

"How else? The same way you know I am Cloe."

"But where? We repeat, where?" In chorus.

"In the smoke and flame, where else?" The woman.

"Ohhh!" In chorus again, through giggles and laughter. "Such fun." The sound of delight gets louder, then dimmer. Suddenly the spotlight goes off and the stage is plunged into darkness. A sound of feet running, scurrying and clattering across stage into the wings.

The stage remains empty for seconds.

Finally, the spotlight goes up on the inner stage. The audience sees a woman with long blond hair down to her waist. But for flowers at her pubic areas and her breasts she seems naked. With her there is a man, but he has long hair too and he is also apparently naked. They carry pole masks, showing greatly distorted faces of painful shame.

"Just because I took a teeney little bite—" The woman in the voice of a shrewish housewife.

"Wonder why the tree bore only one! Seems mighty spooky to me!" He picks at his teeth with a toothpick through the mask's mouth.

"I'll give you spooky. Now whatta we gonna have for supper?"

"Best apple I ever did eat." Cleaning his teeth with a final deft working of the toothpick.

"Didn't even leave the core. Not even a single seed." As the woman is saying the last, the lights dim. The stage becomes dark again and empty for seconds.

Until suddenly, the spotlight floods the inner stage again. Again, a man and woman, somewhat more clothed now. The man's hair is considerably longer than the woman's. The woman's hair is almost a boy's bob.

"I told you. I want it for myself." The woman speaks with impatience, as though to a perverse boy.

"But, to cut it all off! Why? Why, De-lie-ful?" The man caresses his tresses. "It took me so long to grow it and to care for it."

"Oh, you're just like all the rest of them Sammyella—selfish—not a drab of affection in your little finger. The hair—so much—makes you look like some kind of faggot. There I had to say it." Sounding exasperated, yet she pats his long hair lovingly, "Pretty hair, pretty hair. Pretty hair — Oh, so pretty hair—"

"Oh, all right. But don't say I never did anything for you the next time we pass a mink coat display window. Just don't say I never did anything for you."

"You mean it, Sammy?" She is already flourishing a pair of giant scissors. Making practice swipes, she snips the air about his head. A lusty gleam in her eye and a vibratory noise of anticipation in her throat, she goes at his locks. The lights go down rapidly. But the sounds of the giant scissors get louder, become wild. Until suddenly, even the sounds of the scissors stop—leaving a sinister silence. Her voice, finally, gloating, "There—your disguise all gone! You're exposed for what you really are, Samson—just a male chauvinist pig. That's what you get! That's what you deserve! Good enough for-ya! —No consideration for a girl whatsoever!"

"You deceived me, De-lie-ful! You told me a lie! A lie! A lie!" The man shouts.

The woman begins to laugh. As her laugh builds up to uncontrolled delight, then to farouche hysteria, the light goes down.

Again, the stage is absolutely empty for seconds—no sound, sight, or presence.

When the footlights go up again, the audience has a clear view of front stage. A lamp lit at her shoulder, an exotic WOMAN dressed in a negligee sits on a couch, before several T-V sets. SHE is reading a magazine. Ever now and again, SHE looks up to the outer wall of windows which flashes with lights. An electric hammer chuggers intermittently through the sounds coming from the T-V sets. At moments, the chuggering is so strong, no other sounds can be heard. At such moments, THE WOMAN becomes greatly uneasy.

SHE rises and changes magazines. SHE sits down, only to rise a moment later to adjust the floor lamp.

Finally SHE throws the magazine down, rises, gets on stilts and paces. SHE hurries to the window and yanks the curtains across, but there is still so much exposed.

SHE turns the volumes of the T-V sets up full, one after the other. SHE throws

HER arms around one T-V set and puts HER head down on the top, giving HERSELF to the vibrations of the sounds. But when the tripping of the hammer and the flashing occur together, SHE can take no more.

THE WOMAN, "Oh, God! It can't happen again! It just can't!"

She calls out tentatively, "Char!"

SHE hurries to the windows, makes another feeble gesture at the curtains. The flashing and tripping of the hammer continues. "It's no use! There are just too many of them!"

HER voice falls away with desperation. Half running, half falling, SHE moves away from the windows. Sobbing hysterically, SHE gets down from the stilts and sinks to HER knees behind the chairs. For moments SHE is concealed from us. HER sobbing is clearly audible. The exhalations of deep desperation, HER sobbing communicates all the signs and tones of a person who is forced closer and closer to an abyss. The record has stopped playing and the arm goes round and round with the scratchings of a needle running off the grooves.

A knocking at the door left stage interrupts the sobbing. Short and brisk, the knocking incites in THE WOMAN a caught sound of hope almost afraid to express itself. As HER head appears from behind the chairs, we see SHE has stopped crying. As the knocking comes again, THE WOMAN rises. Gasping anxiously, SHE wipes at HER eyes with handkerchief, then dabs at HER face with powder. Primping HER hair nervously, SHE hurries to the door.

Anxiously, trying to reestablish HER customary composure as the knocking comes a third time, "A minute!"

At the door SHE puts the final touches to HER hair. SHE prepares a face to meet the face SHE might meet. Taking the knob, SHE pulls the door open and calls out with desperate hopefulness, "CHAR? Is that you, CHAR?"

A bosomy, hippy YOUNG WOMAN enters. On stilts, she carries a glass of pink liquid.

THE WOMAN, reaching for the glass avidly, "Oh, CHAR! CHAR!"

THE YOUNG WOMAN, "Easy does it, now. Releasing the glass gradually, "You know what happened last time you took it too quickly."

THE WOMAN, "I won't this time, I promise, CHAR. I promise."

SHE takes the glass fully and drinks it as though it were all SHE needed at the moment, nothing else. THE YOUNG WOMAN stands foursquare, adjusting the belt of HER dress.

THE WOMAN, swallowing tentatively, "There, CHAR. It won't happen this time. I won't let it happen." SHE swallows again and again. As SHE does so she reaches out to hold onto the YOUNG WOMAN'S arm.

THE YOUNG WOMAN, "Easy now. Breathe deeply three times."

THE WOMAN, breathing deeply, counts, "One." SHE breathes, "Two." SHE breathes, "Three." SHE breathes. SHE releases THE YOUNG WOMAN's arm tentatively. "There! Bless you, CHAR. You're such a rescue, I don't know what

I'd do without you." She kisses the YOUNG WOMAN on the cheek and puts a hand on THE YOUNG WOMAN's shoulder. THE YOUNG WOMAN slips an arm about her waist. "I can count on you, CHAR. Do YOU know what that means?"

THE WOMAN carrying the glass, THEY walk a little, into the room and about, then back to center stage. THE WOMAN's head rests on THE YOUNG WOMAN's shoulder throughout the walk.

THE YOUNG WOMAN, "Keeping to YOURSELF like that! You ought to join the others in the masquerade party.

What set you off this time?"

THE WOMAN, "I don't know. I just don't know." Turning to the flashing windows, "Aren't they ever going to finish that building? I came here seeking private harbor, and what do I find?" SHE gestures helplessly toward the flashing great window, going rapidly right at that moment. "Fourth of July fireworks and a sleepless lighthouse!" The last with a pathetic laugh.

THE YOUNG WOMAN, "There. There."

THE WOMAN, her eyes turning away from the window, "Aren't they ever going to be done with it. Two years, CHAR. Two years."

THE YOUNG WOMAN, "Seems like no sooner do they rebuild one part they find something else."

THE WOMAN, "They've been at it ever since I got here. Why should they bother me so much today? I guess I've become a ninny, CHAR."

THE YOUNG WOMAN, "At least they were something. Not like the first week when YOU got set off without any reason. As THE GOOD DOCTOR says, progress is on our side."

THE WOMAN, "Oh, CHAR, I am such a ninny. I—feel like old delft crockery put away in the attic. I wait and wait, but no one comes for ME."

THE YOUNG WOMAN, No different from most, I guess. YOU just feel it more."

THE WOMAN, "But YOU, at least, have meaning, CHAR."

THE YOUNG WOMAN, "Meaning? Maybe I do. Like THE GOOD DOCTOR, I guess I can think of YOUR condition as my meaning. But that puts me only one up on YOU."

THE WOMAN, WHO was not listening to the last, "I'm an echo that lost its source."

A group of men and women of various ethnic and racial types, as are all the players in this drama, including THE WOMAN, come on stage. The group is made up of a golden young man, dressed in tunic and barefooted, and four beauties attired in the white folds of Grecian chitons. The four women squabble over the young man until he extricates himself with a spurt to the far stage, left. Breathing hard, he stops and makes a subtle movement of his hand from his hip, "Here, Babies, have a b-a-l-l!" He tosses an apple among them. Squealing, the four women fight each other for the apple, "It's mine!" "It's mine!" "Paree

meant it for me!'' ''Mine!'' ''Mine!'' Hand on hip, Paree sighs with relief and then takes out a pen knife and pares his nails. Seeing the apple roll free of the squabbling women, he bends to it, retrieves it and begins to eat it.
THE YOUNG WOMAN, studying the woman's face, ''There's someone—''
THE WOMAN, still only half hearing, ''I'm the Mary you've forgotten who's atoning for Christ's atonement.'' Then, realizing THE YOUNG WOMAN was about to announce something, ''I'm sorry, CHAR—''
THE YOUNG WOMAN, turning away, deciding the moment is not right, ''No, never mind. Why don't YOU finish your cocktail like a good girl?''
THE WOMAN, HER eyes on the four squabbling masqueraders who are still clawing and struggling on the floor for the ball, ''Ugh, if only it were a cocktail.'' SHE sips the dregs. ''Why should medicine taste as if it should be bad rather than good for you?'' SHE bemuses the glass. ''A way of putting a pleasant taste into medicine would take a fraction of the effort put into perfecting A to Z bombs.'' HER eyes drift back to the tussling women. ''I swear, CHAR—they almost seem—'' And then back to HER glass and THE YOUNG WOMAN. ''Now, CHAR—CHAR, there's a way to win the affection of a man, as we used to say when I was a girl! —Tell him you have an idea that would make him a hero of mankind overnight.'' SHE laughs with tiny pathos.
THE YOUNG WOMAN, laughing openly, ''Win the affection of a man? There's only one way to do that, BABY, and you outta know that by now.'' SHE does a series of grinds and then bump, bump, bump—in time to the flashing at the window and the tripping of the pneumatic hammer. THE YOUNG WOMAN comes up from the bumps and grinds with a nod to THE WOMAN's glass.
THE WOMAN, wise regret in HER voice, ''If only it were that simple —Make OUR lives as WOMEN so much simpler too. SHE downs the last of the dregs with a snapped-on look of great displeasure. ''Always the same'' SHE bemuses the empty glass. ''But always so different.''
THE YOUNG WOMAN, ''Wish one of them different kinds would come this way.''

The squabbling on the floor has moved the women farther and farther offstage. Paree follows after them. From time to time, chomping on the apple with lusty pleasure, he leans over them with a puckish smile while they fight.

With THE YOUNG WOMAN's line, ''Wish one of them different kinds would come this way!'' the squabbling women and Paree finally go off stage left and from offstage, right, a tall bruising man, dressed in short tunic again, pursues a woman onto stage. The man is bald, as though new shaven, and the woman, dressed in long tunic, sports long black tresses, dragging on the stage and sometimes almost tripping her.

So that's why you had me cut my hair!'' The man cries out, his hands reaching as though to yank the hair from the woman's head, which he finally succeeds in doing just before they disappear off stage left, both absolutely bald. Where the man looked bruisingly masquiline bald, because of the shape of his head, the woman looks like a birdling, bald, because her head is knobby and oddly shaped, perhaps even flat on top. As the bald man and woman disappear on the left, from the right emerges a woman, running on stage, carrying a silver platter on which lies a long-haired, bearded man's head, surrounded by parsley, etc. An apple is stuffed in the head's mouth. The woman is pursued by a figure, shoulders high so as to hide the head between built-up shoulder blades. The figure pleads with the woman, its hands agonizing toward the head on the platter, which seems almost to blink an eye and to munch the apple, "Please, Jokey —Don't joke! Give me back my head!" He speaks in the voice of Peter Lorre. With a swing of the platter out of his reach, the woman runs off stage, giggling.

THE WOMAN, Mixed emotions as she glances from the masqueraders to THE YOUNG WOMAN, back to the disappearing masqueraders, then back to THE YOUNG WOMAN again. Finally, SHE draws up close, "Bless you, CHAR. If I had been like you, things might have turned out so much simpler."

THE YOUNG WOMAN, "The ordinary ones don't count —They come and go. But it's the different ones that come on the wings of the—humming bird of love?" SHE speaks with an exaggerated flair as though spoofing a popular song. "Even with them—nothing for any longer than it takes to do it."

THE WOMAN, "There, there, CHAR—patience, my dear. YOU must have patience. A GIRL as Body Beautiful as you, and YOUR whole life still unwalked upon. One day it'll come." As she speaks, a man comes in from right stage. Again, he is dressed like a Greek hero, short tunic, leather thongs about the calves. He is blond and has the arms and legs of a swimmer. With him, a most beautiful girl, perhaps an oriental type (Chinese or Japanese, etc.), dressed in light blue chiton, long tresses free flowing to her hips. Hand on hips, the man speaks, "Look Baby, why don't you be a real—hero—work a little this time around. I'm tired of swimming the Battery— Cry me a puddle, willya?— Later, Wally Rally will use it for his thing with Betty, the Queen."

THE WOMAN, HER eyes following the two disappearing offstage left, only to turn offstage right, where two more masqueraders appear. This time, a young man, this time in toga and a laurel leaf about his head, is dragged on stage by the hand—an older woman, looking like Liz Taylor playing Cleopatra, drags him on, purring, "Come on, Tony—like a good boy. Cleo's got a real feast waiting for you." The young man tries to pull away, "But I'm not hungry."

"But someone else is!" The older woman picks up a tray of fruit. "Here, have an apple—have an orange—have a pomegranate!" She hands him the tray, taking something out of it, all alive and wriggling, as she does, "Oh, look what I found—the apple has a worm. Pretty worm! —Sweet worm! Are you hungry, dear worm? Shall Mommy give you feed? —Ouch! Greedy little baby, isn't he? Here, Tony—the sweet, dear worm!"

"No thanks!" the young man puts up his hand. "Couldn't stand another bite!'' He runs off stage out of the woman's grasp, who takes up a tottering pursuit.

THE WOMAN pulls HER eyes away from the scene reluctantly as though from a grotesque montage that carries hidden meaning for her life. Finally SHE speaks again, ''Dr. Jones? How did you say it was coming with HIM?''

THE YOUNG WOMAN, apparently not much interested in the masquerade scenes as anything more than a costume party, ''DR. JONES?''

THE WOMAN, ''DR. JONES,'' back in the front stage moment, ''DR. MOLLOY — DR. SANTENELLI — DR. RABBINOWITZ—DR. RODRIQUEZ— and now DR. WASHINGTON —'', SHE makes a gesture of insouciance, ''Whoever! How's it coming?''

THE YOUNG WOMAN' ''I'll be checking in with my reports in a few minutes.''

THE WOMAN, significantly, ''That means you'll be along with HIM.''

THE YOUNG WOMAN, offhandedly, ''That means I'll be alone with his pencil and pad —''

THE WOMAN, a little archly and wisely too, ''Many things can happen in fifteen or twenty minutes, the doors closed.''

THE YOUNG WOMAN, ''Where a MAN is concerned, only one thing can happen. With most of THEM it takes much less than fifteen minutes.''

THE WOMAN, laughing, ''CHAR, you're quite priceless. Instead of that ugly tasting medicine, the GOOD DOCTOR ought to send me just YOU, every hour on it, as they say.'' SHE continues to laugh, but only briefly, as the next masquerade unfolds. As the woman in the masquerade reads a long, romantic letter, THE WOMAN becomes serious and appears to be deeply touched. But with the thurst of the last sentence, the very last word, SHE winches and turns away. The masquerade scene consists of a young man and a young woman. The young man is dressed in prisoner's uniform and the woman is dressed in a woman prisoner's dress. The woman reads aloud the letter she has obviously received from the young man, ''Ellie, Darling — Outside my window, I can just hear the sounds of a song bird —As I rise on tip-toe, the bars in my hands, and strain, I can see the bird fluttering in the limbs of the tree in the prison yard — it's a blue bunting — blue like my yearning for you, blue like my heart aching for you — blue, blue, like our love is blue. I think about you the first thing waking up in the morning. I think about you at chow time. I think about you when I work on the marker plates. I think about you at chow time. I think about you when back at my lathe in the afternoon. I think about you at chow time. I think about you in the evening when we watch a film. I think about you at bed-time... But what I want to know now, is, Ellie— Tell me, Ellie, will the world ever let us get to fuck?'' With the last word, THE WOMAN turns her head, as though slapped in the face. SHE seems not to have heard the woman read the letter's closing,''Love, Abbie.'' Recovering, she moans small, ''Oh, Char! Char! What fools! Fools! All of us!'' Her voice catches, ''And what's the use?'' SHE gestures

hopelessly to the masquerade scene, then to the two lovers going off stage separated by the width of the stage, their faces turned yearning to each other, then to the flashing lights in the window, revealing more and more masquerading shadows, and the tripping of the hammer going regularly now.
THE YOUNG WOMAN, as though performing a rescue, "Oh — YOU have a visitor." For minutes, THE WOMAN seems not to have heard. And then, slowly, SHE recovers and looks full to the YOUNG WOMAN. "Says HIS name is DR. DOUGLAS." Expression returns to THE WOMAN's face, disbelief, interest — "Says HIS name is DR. ROBERT DOUGLAS!"
THE WOMAN, a strange sound as of a child moaning piteously small. Finally, recovering, "Are you sure, CHAR? —"
THE YOUNG WOMAN, "That you have a visitor? Of course I'm sure. You think I'm looney too?"
THE WOMAN, unhearing, self-absorbed in hushed disbelief, "ROBERT DOUGLAS?" Her voice quavers.
THE YOUNG WOMAN, "That's what he says his name is —"
THE WOMAN, "ROBERT DOUGLAS, here — to see ME? —"
THE YOUNG WOMAN, matter of fact, "Here. See for yourself—" SHE makes a move as though to go off stage.
THE WOMAN, puts her hand on the YOUNG WOMAN's arm, "No wait —" musing aloud, "I knew — I just knew — All morning, all day, everything I did, everything I touched seemed — more than itself."
THE YOUNG WOMAN, "You want me to have HIM sent up?"
THE WOMAN, "What? Oh, yes, send HIM up...CHAR —" The YOUNG WOMAN pauses in the doorway — "Give me a few minutes?"
THE YOUNG WOMAN, with a wink and o.k. sign, "Will do!" SHE backs out the door snappily.
THE WOMAN, as the door closes, HER hand going to HER forehead, fluttering lightly. "ROBERT DOUGLAS." HER voice diminishing small!, "ROBERT — DOUGLAS!" And then to the closed door, a tiny plea, "CHAR! — don't leave me alone—with him!" SHE looks about frantically until SHE finds HER bathrobe and, yanking it on, falls into an easy chair to recover. A moment later, an afterthought, SHE rises and hurries to a wall mirror where she applies lipstick, pats hair into place, primps and straightens HER dress robe. SHE starts to hum a tune, then gives it up. SHE goes to the settee and pumps out the pillows, picks up books, newspapers, and magazines, and arranges them in the magazine rack and the bookcase. As the room begins to look what SHE considers presentable, HER composure begins to return. Almost entirely herself again, SHE gives off an aura of a great effort of will being made as SHE answers the knocking at the door.

Throughout the following scene, up to the moment THE WOMAN and THE MAN begin to act out the past, Cassy and Damn John, each carrying handmasks stretched into extravagantly lewd faces, parade about the inner stage with one woman after another (each of these wearing masks of vacuous expressions), which women they swap frequently one at a time and by twos and threes, until they run through every available woman on stage and, about to turn, at the same moment, to THE WOMAN, ready to fight over her like dogs over a last bone left, think better of it and, instead, turn to each other. As they are warming up to each other, Martin Luther comes on stage, walking arm in arm with his wife, gently conversing — at which sight, Cassy says whiningly to Damn John, "Of all women, a nun turns me on the least. The withdrawal of their flesh, you know — like opening up a closet of mothballs!" He bends to Damn John and takes a nip of his ear lobe.

Also, through this act, once Cassy and Damn John play out their scene, little groups of the masqueraders file on and off stage, doing their thing, improvising. Every now and again THEY turn to watch the action between THE WOMAN and THE MAN unfold itself. As the action between THE WOMAN and THE MAN becomes more dramatic and more compelling, they move slowly farther and farther into the front stage area, until they are gathered about the TWO as a second audience, as it were, an on-stage audience. When the drama between THE WOMAN and THE MAN becomes so compelling, as in the third act, the masqueraders disappear as masqueraders and remain on stage as the second audience. All scenes between THE MAN and THE WOMAN when THEY are not sitting down and are also in the present are on stilts, when possible.

THE WOMAN, as she opens the door and THE MAN enters, on stilts, "ROBERT — ROBERT —" But HER voice breaks off.

THE MAN, "MELISSANDA." HE speaks the name as though it carries many echoes from the past. HIS entrance seems to have been worried about and rehearsed.

THE WOMAN puts her hand out as though to fend the moment as much as to offer HER hand to him.

THE MAN, taking HER hand, "MELISSANDA!"

THE WOMAN, her composure returning with it, "You're a sight for — old eyes. ROBERT DOUGLAS." Still fighting her feelings.

THE MAN, smiling a little too brilliantly, "MELISSANDA, you're still the best looking girl ever!"

THE WOMAN, giving him a look, "No, you haven't changed. You still can't see what's plain to your eyes."

THE MAN, "Eyes, MELISSA? — Heart's eyes!" As though reciting from the past.

THE WOMAN, looking at him quickly, "Heart's eyes?" And then away. "You still remember!"

THE MAN, "MELISSANDA — I — I —"

THE WOMAN, back in the moment, "Feel sorry for me? Is that what you feel?" Gaily, forced, "No — Don't Robert — Don't ever feel sorry for ME." SHE glances apprehensively at the windows.

THE MAN, speaking as SHE returns from a few steps about the room, to the record player to turn off the machine, then back to HIM, "MELISSANDA — I — all I was going to say is it's — so good to see you, and be near you again."

THE WOMAN, "Be near me again, ROBERT?"

THE MAN, "To be close to you and feel YOU."

THE WOMAN, "I'm wrong — YOU have changed."

THE MAN, "Changed? How?"

THE WOMAN, getting a hold of herself. "Yes, changed. Remember how it was with ME — even when I was just a little girl who was not afraid to show her knees and, when she fell, her something more? — Looking forward to the time when it wouldn't be right for me to go around showing off my knees and my something more, even when I fell down, all I dreamed of was a house, my house. Remember how the others used to make fun of me? Pointing to a garage, pointing to a chicken coop, they cried, 'Melissanda, look — look — there's your house!' And I would cry and think to MYSELF, Someday — someday they'll see! But you didn't know the last, did YOU, Robert? — that I cried and had such thoughts?" SHE gives him a token glance.

THE MAN, the echo of a sheepish grin slips uneasily into HIS face, "Yes, you were always — so patient."

THE WOMAN, giving a light, SELF-spoofing laugh, "Not really, ROBERT, dear. It was just MY way of adjusting to things I could not have. Patience is the name WE give to things WE want now but cannot have until WE no longer want them."

The air is cleared with their laughter.

THE MAN, "I take it back — you have changed. You were never exactly what might be called a witty person."

THE WOMAN, giving HIM a look, "No — YOU were the witty one, weren't YOU? Remember that song YOU made up — about me and MY house?" SHE begins to hum. Slowly one word catches another, one pulling the other out of HER memory mood. SHE sings:

See, see the house that Robbie built—
This is the roof that covers the house that Robbie built;
These are the walls that hold up the roof
that covers the house that Robbie built;
This is the floor that's under the walls that hold up the roof
That covers the house that Robbie built;
And Melissanda's the girl that wants to walk on the floor
That's under the walls
That holds up the roof
That covers the house that Robbie built. . . . .

Rocking rhythmically, SHE repeats some of the lines; the words trail away. "Oh, yes, — YOU were the clever one. It was only in your ditties that YOU let yourself be caught."

As SHE sings, ROBERT looks progressively more uncomfortable. The prevailing mood is one of regret, lost dreams and vanished youth. The stage lights dim. A small spotlight comes slowly across the stage and fixes the telephone. In seconds, *the telephone becomes a great, dominating presence. Rising from the settee and skipping like a little girl, she goes to the phone, takes the receiver up in both hands. She presses the receiver to one and then the other ear.*

In a shy, demure voice, an ideal little girl's voice, THE WOMAN,

Hello — This is Melissanda Mink.
Robert Douglas? —Robbie? Hello, Robbie —
You can call me Melissa —
When grownups are around, Melissanda, it seems.
Just today? You moved in just today?
Oh, yesterday — but today you ate your first dinner here —
Tonight you have your first sleep here?
Yes, yes — I'll ask Mother. But I'm sure she'll say
'Yes.' I'll go and ask her and then change my dress.

She replaces the phone on the saddle, again with both hands. Sighing lightly, she sits back and folds her hands, like a cup in her lap. As she sits, quiet, reposed, demure, for seconds, the lights dim again. When the light at the settee goes up again, the telephone is in its place, but now it is just another stage prop. THE WOMAN is seen returning to the settee, to the man. THE MAN is puzzled and awed, also somewhat shamefaced.

THE WOMAN smiles graciously, "But — you know — so many good things have been happening to you. I've been reading about you in the papers, Robert." SHE sits down and gives him the attention of her face.

THE MAN, recovering, his mood momentarily bouyant. But HIS learned reserve and modesty rise to smother HIS buoyancy, "It's nothing, really — just MY work — MY way of earning rights to MY daily cubic allotment of oxygen on the face of this overcrowded earth."

THE WOMAN, "YOU know that's not right. YOU were always one to give more than was really asked of YOU, even in school."

THE MAN, self-effacing, "Yes, YOU had patience, and I — I guess I had the worm — for books. It was just, just MY way of showing everyone else I was worth something too, even though I could never stunt the leader —"

THE WOMAN, a soft knowing look through HER smile, "Your MOTHER? How is YOUR mother, ROBERT?"

THE MAN, looking at HER, "Funny YOU should bring HER up at this moment. While I was talking, I found myself thinking about HER." HE looks at HER with wonder and an aura of witnessing a revelation.

THE WOMAN, showing not a change of emotion, "How is SHE, ROBERT? It's been so long, you know."

THE MAN, "YOU don't know? No, I guess YOU wouldn't. SHE —she's been gone six weeks now."

THE WOMAN, with regret and something else, something almost personal, subjective, "Dead? Oh, I'm so sorry. You —" Something in THE MAN's face stops HER.

THE MAN, "Not at all. It was best — for both of US — the only way out for both of US. To paraphrase the bard, SHE should have died long since —"

THE WOMAN, gives him a look, "Don't say that. SHE had everything to live for."

THE MAN, "Yes, long since. It would have been better for both of US."

THE WOMAN, visibly rattled, though SHE fights for composure, "Is there a MRS. DOUGLAS? Married, ROBERT?" Hesitation in HER voice, "Is ROBERT DOUGLAS married?"

THE MAN, with a cough, "No, — not married."

THE WOMAN, "What a pity! But YOU always were too clever to be caught, weren't YOU?" Again, a tone of slight hesitancy.

THE MAN, with real regret, almost self-pity in HIS voice, "I'd say not clever enough to permit myself to be caught."

THE WOMAN, banteringly, "Oh, YOU don't mean that, ROBERT —"

THE MAN, his emotions full in HIS face, "I do — not clever enough to permit MYSELF to be caught, as YOU put it."

THE WOMAN, looks at HIM reflectively, "You know, WE patients call this a rest home. But it's really a haven for alcoholics and people who have nervous breakdowns."

THE MAN, "Yes, yes — but does it matter?"

THE WOMAN, still looking at HIM, "You ever hear of charade therapy: acting out OUR fears and bad memories. It helps so, especially when done in groups. Sometimes WE act out dreams and hopes — but these are lonely, individual matters, more difficult to control... Will YOU do a charade with me, ROBERT?"

THE MAN, puzzled, "Charades? Here? With YOU now?"

THE WOMAN, "YOU have no idea, the sense of cleansing, of well-being. It's just like regular charades, just like the game — only YOU speak, too."

THE MAN, taken by the spirit of play as a way over an embarrassing moment, "Play charades? Haven't done this since — Oh, yes," smiling with light ribaldry, "Alex Dwight's stag party — crazy party!"

THE WOMAN, "Will YOU — will YOU do one with ME, ROBERT?"

THE MAN, "Sure, it'll be fun. MELISSA, it'll be fun to play charades with YOU."

THE WOMAN, "Really so simple, ROBERT. You'll see.

The stage is blacked out. And then a spotlight, defining everything overclearly, holds the center of the stage. In the spot we see the woman and the man, in the attitude of little children, stooping to play a game. They appear about twelve or thirteen.

THE MAN, speaking, ululating in an inciting little boy's voice, "It's your turn, Melissanda. Spin the bottle — Spin the bottle, Melissanda."

THE WOMAN, shy, hesitant, looking about herself, "Robbie."

THE MAN, "Go ahead, Melissanda — it's your turn to be kissed. Spin the bottle, Melissanda."

THE WOMAN, finally spinning the imaginary bottle, she waits with her hands clasped, shyly, almost prayerfully, "Oh — it's you." With both large hesitancy and unmistakable joy, "The bottle's pointing to you."

THE MAN, in a raucous, taunting boy's voice as he moves quickly to one side, "No, it isn't Melissanda. It isn't really. See, it isn't really pointing at me. Go ahead, spin the bottle — Spin the bottle, Melissanda —"

THE WOMAN, just sits, hesitant, incomplete as the man's voice goes on with its boy's taunt, "Go ahead, quick — Spin the bottle, Melissanda. Melissanda, it's your turn to be kissed." The spotlight snaps off. The light at the settee goes up. We discover THE MAN and THE WOMAN again seated on the settee. THE WOMAN is sighing, and the look of compassion on THE MAN's face is unmistakable. Remembering THEY are back in the present, HE turns to the woman with an interested smile. Compassion is still in HIS face. THE WOMAN speaks with pity, love, and regret!

"They were so innocent, helpless, and — inexperienced. Most of the time they had to make their own way in life. Even when they were given directions, it was not always the right kind. Poor creatures, if they had only known what WE know now —

THE MAN, making a movement toward HER, "Yes — if they had only known."

THE WOMAN, she looks at HIM and then returns to HER former composure, "Your important work, Robert — about which I read so much in the papers — tell me about it."

THE MAN, looks at HER, hesitant, then gives in to HER gambit, "Not so important, really. The new nuclear project."

HIS voice diminishes, the lights go down. *The spotlight again makes the telephone the dominating stage presence. Rising, the woman is now not so much the little girl on the threshold of puberty as she is a growing up young lady of fifteen or sixteen. Answering the insistence of the telephone, she shifts the receiver from ear to ear still, yet with more grace, less excitement.*

THE WOMAN, in the voice of a sixteen year old, pie and ice cream girl:

Yes, Robbie — This is she — I — Melissa —
The poem you wrote me was, oh, so sweet —
So sweet it was to read. Be your best girl at the party?
I can't say no — If Mummy will let me go —

Will say yes; just give me time to change my dress.

Returning the receiver to the saddle, she sits back with a deep sign and spreads an imaginary scrap of paper before herself. The spot going off, the telephone again recedes. The settee light goes up, revealing THE MAN again, perplexed, troubled, as THE WOMAN, HER former self, comes walking to him.

THE WOMAN, WE do it all the time. It helps. YOU see it helps, don't YOU?''

THE MAN, afraid to look at HER directly, ''Yes, it helps. As YOU say, sense of well-being.'' With the last, HE looks into HER face as though afraid of what HE might see.

THE WOMAN, stretching, ''Nothing like it really — not even sleep in childhood or a hot bath in adolescence.''

THE MAN, HIMSELF, again, giving a soft throaty laugh, ''Yes. HE also stretches HIS arms.

THE WOMAN, still stretching, ''Go ahead — go ahead — it's really the best thing for YOU right now. It's like a follow through in dancing.'' THEY stretch and sigh deeply. Finally THE WOMAN settles on the settee again, ready to lead THEIR old-friends' chat, but now warmed by an echo of THEIR past feeling. ''Well, now — Shall WE go on with our visit?''

THE MAN, with ingenuous wonder, ''YOU have changed. I thought I knew just about all sides of YOU.''

THE WOMAN, reflectively, a little sadly, ''That was one of the troubles with US — In some ways WE knew each other too well —'' SHE pulls herself up again. ''But now about YOUR work again — NUCLEAR PHYSICS, isn't it?''

THE MAN, ''Yes, NUCLEAR PHYSICS — uninspired, unimaginative, depriving man of his last romantic footing on this earth.''

THE WOMAN' ''Uninspired? Unimaginative? Not THE ROBBIE DOUGLAS I knew.''

THE MAN, ''Perhaps this was one of the ways WE didn't know each other.''

THE WOMAN, ''Maybe — I remember when I first learned YOU were going into physics — the last week in high school — how disappointed I felt. I asked YOU why. And YOU said —''

THE MAN, in the voice of a high school boy justifying his choice, *''And I said, I don't know — I just want to do it — because maybe when I am doing an experiment, everything under my fingertips, for the first time I feel I really count, like a football star or the class president.'' And then in the voice of a grownup man, his natural voice, ''Yes, that's it. In the laboratory, I can control things, I can change them the way I want them to be. Yes, that's it — everything seems no longer elusive and uncertain, everything under control: microscope to scales, scales to rack and to paper and mathematical solution. Gives man the feel of being in the saddle for the first time, answerable to no one but himself . . .*

''On top of that, the sense of adventure. YOU were right — there is

adventure and poetry to nuclear physics — the adventure of the unknown, the poetry of the rhythm of laboratory procedure and an experiment moving along, with the imagination prodding THE UNKNOWN in the ribs until it's out in the open.

"And the feeling! It's like driving an automobile a hundred and twenty miles an hour on a wide-open desert straightaway, and the wheel always answering the touch of your hands. It's — it's like nothing you'll ever know anywhere alse again, and you know it."

THE WOMAN, WHO has been watching HIM all this time, "Yes, not at all uninspired, unimaginative — not ROBERT DOUGLAS, not my ROBBIE DOUGLAS." The last is said in a voice falling away into a little girl's. The lights going down after it, the spotlight goes up like the reversed swing of a pendulum. THE MAN and WOMAN are again revealed, this time on the threshold of manhood and womanhood. THE WOMAN speaks with the voice of a girl in her late teens.

THE WOMAN; "Here for you, Robbie. Happy — happy everyday!"

THE MAN, "A birthday present!"

THE WOMAN, "Go on — open it, Robbie!"

THE MAN, opening the present, "A book of poetry!" (with pleasure). "A — Bible?" Perplexity, perhaps disappointment.

THE WOMAN, "The book of poetry is because I want you not ever to change — The Bible — to remind you there's someone always bigger — taking care of both of us."

THE MAN, a little caustically, "Oh, I see." They walk along quietly for minutes. Finally the woman speaks.

THE WOMAN, "I don't know what to do, Robbie. Mother says it would be best to go to Smith and from there right to the graduate school of social work. They say it's the best in the country. But Wellesley is a good school, too, for what I want —"

THE MAN, "Go to Wellesley. You'll be happier there — better school and all that —"

THE WOMAN, hope and relief of a teen age girl, "Then you do want me nearby."

THE MAN, "I didn't say that. Oh, I'll be glad to have a friend a bicycle ride away from tech —"

THE WOMAN, "You do want me to go to Wellesley. You do. Just say it, Robbie."

THE MAN, determinedly, "I didn't say that. I didn't say that at all — a friend nearby, that's all."

The spotlight goes off, then up again to indicate a change of scene and time. We discover THE WOMAN and THE MAN again, two undergraduates, a boy and a girl, out on a walking date. There is a sense of Spring swelling in the air.

THE MAN, sniffing the air, "Ummmm — the night."
THE WOMAN, "It does smell good, doesn't it? It's like — I don't know — what is it like, Robbie?"
THE MAN, quickly, easily, "It's like a scene from Faust. And you," smiling at her, "you're my Margaret — Oh, linger awhile/so fair thou art."
THE WOMAN, moving closer to his side, "You're so poetic tonight."
THE MAN, slipping his arm about her waist, his face turning to give itself to hers, "You, my Margaret — No, my Melissanda. And I your Palleas."

They stop. The moment is filled with awesome expectations. The woman stands with her head hanging and the man watches her as though he were frightened of something in the moment, in himself. Moving abruptly, awkwardly, he puts his arms about her and begins to embrace her. They embrace passionately. Groping at each other, they sink to the ground. The spotlight snaps off. When the full stage lights go up, with the floor lamp at the settee, the MAN and the WOMAN on the settee now seem to have been touched deeply by the last scene. It is as though THEY had witnessed something that could never again be, therefore precious.

THE WOMAN, with a sigh, "Youth — Innocent, carefree youth. Nothing as important as the moment itself, nothing quite as long."
THE MAN, visibly touched, "Was it that long ago? — First found and lost back there?"
THE WOMAN, "Not really lost, Robert. With YOU nothing was ever really lost — not so long as YOU wrote poetry. Remember?"
THE MAN, thinking hard, "Was it after that time?"
THE WOMAN, "Yes. Robert?"
THE MAN, making a great effort to remember, "Let me think — Hmmmm — "
THE WOMAN, "Recite it, Robert."
THE MAN, dropping HIS head into HIS hands, "Oh, God!"
THE WOMAN, "You remember."
THE MAN, "I can't! I can't! It was so long ago."
THE WOMAN, "Yes, you can. Just think — think."
THE MAN, "I can't! I can't!"
THE WOMAN, a tolerant, understanding smile like a mother who recognizes her little boy's limitations and accepts them, "Just like a MAN — no memory — for the important things. It goes:

This, now, your life's warm modality:
Smile soft, hair soft, and flesh soft.
Near you it is always springtime in my love —

Here, let ME get it. It's tucked away in the drawer of the magazine rack. Looking at it just the other day —"

THE MAN raises HIS head, a small light of something like hope in HIS eyes as

HE watches HER. All the while SHE is walking from the settee to the magazine rack and hunting out the poem, SHE continues reciting. The paper discovered and taken in hand, SHE goes on reading without a break as SHE walks back. SHE recites the last line:

"This, now, your life's warm modality:
Smile soft, hair soft, and flesh soft.
Near you it is always springtime in my love —
The sudden grass, greener still with morning's quiet
exhalations;
The slow unfurling of line, image and rhythm in day's
first yearnings;
The flight of the ardor bird from limb to limb to nest;
And, then, suddenly, under me, you, quite new."

(THE MAN joins her here)

I have known the suns of morning's conjugation,
Grass to grass, trunk yearning up into branch,
And branch unfolding leaf, opening leaf upn opening leaf
Until neither grass, trunk, branch, nor opening leaf alone
Could urge — could start — could move,
Until suddenly now, it is full noon.

(THE MAN drops out)

And now again soft is our yearning,
Flesh soft, hair soft, and smile soft;
Springhour urges know summer's long suspiration —
The ardor bird squats resting in its nest;
Rhythm, image and line become heart's full-toned satiety;
The ruffle mane of grass is one slow chorus of mute
benediction,
Saying, 'Ave, Ave — the day is done.' Come, now, the day
is just begun."

As SHE reads, the MAN watches HER with reawakened hope. When SHE finishes, SHE looks at HIM with a smile, "There, the poem."

THE MAN, "Quite a good college try, even though I say so myself."

THE WOMAN, humorously on the defensive, protective of the poem, "Of course it is — for anybody. The girl to whom it was written was just not worthy of it."

THE MAN, protesting too loudly, as though trying to make up for something in which HE was remiss in the past, "Oh, no — The poem was not good enough for her. No, No, MELISSANDA — don't ever think or say that."

THE WOMAN, smiling with quiet composure, "Why not? It was the truth, wasn't it? WE both knew that. How together we were night birds, shunning the light of day. YOU seemed to be two things to me — How WE responded to each other at night, in the shadows of the campus trees and hills; the plain distance between US during the daytime. YOU seemed to shun taking me anywhere until after dark. Even then, WE never seemed to go anywhere other students might go. Of course I began to suspect the truth, that YOU weren't really proud of ME as a — woman — that YOU were ashamed to have ME known among your friends as YOUR girl."

THE MAN, with a sense of real anguished compassion, "Oh, no — You mustn't ever think that." But the WOMAN isn't listening. HER eyes are turned dreamily to the telephone again. The lights go down. The spot fixes the telephone. *The WOMAN rises from her chair and walks to the telephone like a twenty- or twenty-one year old young lady. She keeps alternating the phone receiver from ear to ear, now with more grace. She speaks in the voice of a poised young lady who has a knowledge of love, of affection deeply returned to herself.*

THE WOMAN:

Hello. Hello. Yes, yes, Robbie darling — oh, darling,
Of course, darling — Of course. Lead
With you the grand march? Oh, yes, darling, yes — (a sharp knocking
Just give me a moment to change my — at the door.)

A man's voice over the P.A. system, commanding, like a scolding parent. "Melissanda! Melissanda Mink!"

The side door opens simultaneously. A harsh light from the corridor intrudes into the telephone scene, a visual harmony of the harsh P.A. voice. Holding a glass with the pink liquid, the YOUNG WOMAN stands in the doorway. The telephone dangling in HER hand, the WOMAN stares about herself and upwards and then into the doorway, uncomprehending, yet HER face reveals guilt.

The YOUNG WOMAN speaks to the P.A. system, off hand but with deference, taking charge, "It's O.K., Sir. I'll be able to handle this."

THE YOUNG WOMAN, leaning against the jambs of the doorway, "I knocked three times and no one seemed to answer." Then actually seeing THE WOMAN for the first time, understanding, "My poor little girl — at it again. YOU know you shouldn't — It excites YOU so much." SHE walks across the stage, takes the receiver from THE WOMAN's hand and places it back on the saddle. SHE speaks to THE MAN, "Please turn up the light." Then to THE WOMAN, her voice soft and tender in reprimanding, "YOU know how much they take out of YOU, Baby."

THE MAN turns up the light and then rises as though to go to THE WOMAN.

THE WOMAN, shaken up but trying to smile wanly to the YOUNG WOMAN, "CHAR — you're so good for me — so, so kind."

THE YOUNG WOMAN, still softly reprimanding, "You know they're not good for you — Why do YOU do it?" To THE MAN, "You shouldn't encourage HER to do this unsupervised."

THE WOMAN, "I thought they were just like the charades."

THE YOUNG WOMAN, "Oh, no — not the same, and YOU know it. Here now, just sit back. After a while WE'LL have cocktails, shall WE?"

THE WOMAN, "Good, kind CHAR. YOU understand so much."

Throughout the scene between THE WOMAN and THE NURSE, THE MAN looks on with anguished compassion and a sense of personal frustration. THE WOMAN sits back for seconds while THE YOUNG WOMAN stands over HER, waiting with the glass held out. Finally THE WOMAN takes the glass and goes on, sighing, her composure returning. "There. Shall I have my cocktail, now?" SHE takes the medicine and sips it just as though it were a cocktail. "How is it coming along? —With Dr. Robbinowitz — Dr. Rodriguez? —Which?"

THE YOUNG WOMAN, DR. RODRIGUEZ! — It was ROBBINOWITZ yesterday. Today is another today. I've just about given HIM up for lost. HE'S one of those intense kind — YOU know — wears glasses because HE has to. Keeps talking about pictures, paintings, I mean and music, classical, all the time during cigarette breaks. WE're just two different worlds. I'm just not good enough for HIM, and I might as well admit it —"

THE WOMAN, reaching out to nurse, "Oh, no, CHAR —don't ever think that!" Remembering the very same words had been said by someone else, and in that room, to HER, SHE stops. SHE puts HER hand to HER forehead as though HER head ached.

THE YOUNG WOMAN, HER body riding with the exaggerated lilt, carrying the aura of a spoof, "Oh, well — I'm not worried. At least there's always one thing WE're compatible in. Should be enough to keep us together for a couple dates, anyways — if HE ever gets around to asking me."

While THE YOUNG WOMAN speaks, the MAN watches with a light dilemma of fascination and wonder.

THE WOMAN, drinking quickly, as though to get it over with, "CHAR — Oh, well, it's medicine — got to be taken for the good that will come after it."

THE YOUNG WOMAN, one tracked, "Oh, well — it's life — reality, as some of those young interns say. Might as well face it."

The exaggerated, self-spoofing lilt throbs through HER body.

THE END OF STAGE ONE

Stage II

A week later. THE MAN and THE WOMAN on the terrace to the rest home. On THEIR left, the rest room with its great window. On THEIR right, the building going up, workers crawling over the structure on all sides with acetylene torches and pneumatic drills. The flashing of the torches and the chuggering of the drills are louder than in the first act, of course. Somehow, however, THE WOMAN notices them less. Throughout this act, CHAR passes by in the background accompanied by a series of MEN in white coats.

THE WOMAN, "I'm happy you came back, ROBERT. It tells ME YOU don't come here out of mere pity."

THE MAN, "Pity, MELISSA — If so, then it's for MYSELF."

THE WOMAN, "YOU miss YOUR MOTHER that much? Yes, I guess YOU would."

THE MAN, "I can't help MYSELF — Whatever I do, whatever I think —"

THE WOMAN, "Yes, YOUR MOTHER had a way with a MAN —"

THE MAN, "MOTHER was everything the world expected of a WOMAN. That was why it was so hard to get angry when I really felt angry with HER, to keep things from HER when I felt the need for a life of MY own. A MAN begins to mistrust his instincts. HE thinks something is wrong with him to want to shut out a WOMAN so good. Also, it was so hard to let HER down in the expectations SHE had of life, for ME. It seemed the greatest cruelty to have let such a woman down. SHE had given so much of the best in herself, above and beyond, as THEY say, for those SHE loved."

THE WOMAN, again smiling HER agreement and understanding, "Yes, that was YOUR mother — daring to be entirely a WOMAN."

THE MAN, "That's a curious way of putting it. Why do YOU say that?"

THE WOMAN, "ROBERT," placing HER hand on HIS arm and smiling smartly as though about to divulge something half in seriousness and half in humor, "I'm going to reveal to YOU a FEMALE secret that's been passed down from MOTHER to DAUGHTER to GRANDDAUGHTER ever since Eve. YOU're probably the first man to hear this. Lucky for US, YOU men are so preoccupied in trying to avoid finding out about YOURSELVES, YOU never get around to finding out anything about US.

"Under the skin of all HER wiles and coquetry, more than anything else, what a WOMAN really wants is to throw HERSELF away. Now on a hat, now on a new really daring recipe — but always, most completely, on a MAN. All SHE asks in return is that SHE be permitted to wear the hat whenever SHE has the whim, and that it flatter HER; that HER recipe turn out right, that it be enjoyed and appreciated; and that THE MAN permit himself to be loved by HER. As I say, it is OUR way — the only way WE can take a firm hold on life. WE think that by spoiling the things WE love, OUR chances of keeping them longer are made better.

"Nowadays, a WOMAN needs a great deal of courage to dare this old fashioned chance. YOUR MOTHER had this courage. Sure, SHE knew there were risks, to HERSELF and to the ONE SHE loved. But also, SHE felt her love and what SHE had to offer were great enough to make up for almost everything. Truth to tell, it just had to be that way. It was the only way SHE could find happiness.

THE MAN, highly attentive to the moment, "Why didn't it come out right with US, MELISSANDA? WE had so much feeling for EACH OTHER, so much to offer EACH OTHER. Was it my MOTHER?"

THE WOMAN, "Oh, I'm not going to let myself be put in the position of having to go after MOTHER. SHE's enough of a goat, poor darling. Let the world go on to the next. Let's face it, ROBERT — it's a man's world, and whenever anything happens to make things turn out not just right, the first thing you men do is holler, 'MOTHER', even if only to curse HER. Nowadays, 'MOTHER' is the name we give the bad things that happened to us in OUR childhood."

THE MAN, "Yes, yes — YOU have changed — so sharp of wit."

THE WOMAN, not rising to the sincere flattery, "It's living alone that does it. A WOMAN learns to keep herself entertained — talking to HERSELF," noticing the hesitant, queer look THE MAN gives her, "interior talking — like playing solitaire."

THE MAN, serious again, "Then what was it? What do YOU think went wrong between US, MELISSA?"

THE WOMAN, looking at HIM quickly with a soft catch in HER throat as SHE speaks, "I haven't heard myself being called that by YOU — since —"

THE MAN, moving toward HER as though to embrace HER, "Oh, MELISSA! MELISSA!" HE compromises the moment by putting HIS hand on HER arm.

THE WOMAN, neither encouraging nor discouraging the gesture, "All those days alone, nothing is missed so much as the presence of a MAN, just to be touched by HIM. And then, when it finally happens, well there it is — just another thing. You wonder what made you want it so strongly to begin with."

THE MAN, deeply stirred, "MELISSA! MELISSA! It's still —" He actually attempts to embrace HER softly, but there's more compassion than passion in the gesture.

THE WOMAN, as though stirred from a trance, moving lightly away from HIM, aborting HIS attempt, "What went wrong between us? I don't know. Do you think it was one thing? Yes, I guess it'll have to be — one thing, or two or three simple, easily understood —"

THE MAN, "MELISSA — I —"

THE WOMAN, smiling tenderly, "Poor dear — Just like YOU, so afraid of disturbing anyone. That was always your dilemma, YOU know, always having to decide between hurting yourself and someone close to YOU. Don't worry, YOU really needn't be concerned — I don't mind talking about these things. They've become well-worn, china cups, ready and friendly to the hand."

THE MAN, hesitantly, afraid HE might be prying. HE is perhaps also uneasy with the idea that MELISSANDA might have discussed HIM with HER doctor, "You mean as part of your daily life in the home?"

THE WOMAN, "Oh, as that too. Talking things out, we call it. I've found it to be one of the best possible things. PEOPLE should try it more often. YOU have no idea how misunderstandings can be cleared away, just by two PEOPLE sitting down and talking about them. An unhappy thing about the kind of world WE live in is that the wisdom and ability to talk things out come so late in life, and then it's often too late. That was one of OUR difficulties — WE were never able to talk things out. WE always let emotions lead US by the nose."

With the last, the lights go down on the stage. Seconds later, the spotlight snaps on center stage. We discover *the man and the woman, college students, in an attitude of emotional disturbance, a sense of hopelessness, indecision.*

THE MAN, *as a deeply agitated youth, wanting to do the right thing but not knowing where it lay, he knows something, right or wrong, has to be done, "It's taking — too much time. I don't know what to do — I just can't afford to take so much time off from my work in the laboratory."*

THE WOMAN, *a hesitant, hurt, and uncertain young lady, "Is that all it is to you, like something on scales or under a microscope, to be measured?"*

THE MAN, *desperate, immensely unhappy because he again has to make a choice, and then attempt to carry it off well, "You're just making it harder for me, Melissa. You know I can't afford to spend so much time with you. I have the assistantship to live up to."*

THE WOMAN, *on the verge of quiet tears, "I — don't know what to say — Robbie —"*

THE MAN, *speaking with determination now, "We've been seeing too much of each other — for both our good. I have my work to think of — and you —"*

THE WOMAN, *tears in her eyes, "You think that, Robbie?"*

THE MAN, *fighting to keep his voice determined, "We should date others. It's not natural for two people to see so much of each other for so many years. We've come to depend on each other too much, Melissa. It's gotten so the one of us can't think about anything or do anything without thinking of the other."*

THE WOMAN, *putting her head on his chest — her tears coming silently, "Oh, Robbie! Sometimes I'm so afraid."*

THE MAN, *swept up by her emotions, he puts his arms around her, "Oh, Melissa! Melissa!"*

THE WOMAN, *pressing herself closer to him, her arms about his neck, the weight of her body against him, "Robbie! Darling! — Oh, Robbie!"*

They embrace passionately. Full and easily fallen into, not fumbling and aimless like the last, their embrace is still somewhat desperate and hopeless as they lie down together on the stage.

The spotlight goes off. The stage lights and the floor lamp at the settee go up — we see THE WOMAN and THE MAN seated again. THEY seem deeply moved by the charade scene. During the last minute of action, THE MAN has taken THE WOMAN's hand. HE clutches HER hand tightly.

THE MAN, with awe, as though HE had just witnessed something forbidden and holy, "Was it then, you think?"

THE WOMAN, "What?" And then giving HIM a tender smile and squeezing HIS hand, "It must have been then. You were so — sweet."

THE MAN, falling into her mood, "Yes, it must have been then. I don't think I shall ever forget that night, in spite of the feeling of hopelessness that came before."

THE WOMAN, holding HIS hand now, "Yes, it's one of those things WE understand so late about the world. So often things that are the sweetest are preceded by unnecessary heartaches." A sad afterthought, "Too often they are also followed by even more pain."

THE MAN, the remark striking home, "Yes, we were careless — weren't we?"

THE WOMAN, making naught of the whole thing with a light tutting, "Such things happen. WE took so much happiness out of time." SHE looks away from HIM for just a brief moment.

Once again the lights go down. The spotlight fixes center stage and *the man and the woman, a youth and young lady again, two months after the previous scene. Sitting in hard-back chairs as though in a booth in a cocktail lounge or bar, they linger over drinks. They seem to be watching dancing couples, watching and listening to a jazzband. Every now and again, Melissanda turns to him and watches his face, as though trying to make up her mind about something.*

THE WOMAN, *"Robbie."*

THE MAN, *his eyes turned away from the moment in the booth, "There's something about people on a dance floor and together at a cocktail bar! They seem to weave tents about themselves, shutting themselves off from the rest of the world."*

THE WOMAN, *a little more determination in her voice, "Robbie."*

THE MAN, *his attention returned, his eyes on her, "I'm sorry, Melissa, I didn't mean to be rude."*

THE WOMAN, *a smile of understanding, "It's all right. I like to watch people, too — especially when they're together."*

THE MAN, *sensing more is intended than met his ears, "A woman's viewpoint."*

Making a broad joke of it, "I guess it'll always be that way — you holding the woman's and I, the man's viewpoint. Strange isn't it?"

THE WOMAN, *smiling, yet looking for things in his face, "Crazy, intellectual tech. genius. I guess you'll always be that way —"*

THE MAN, *with mock seriousness, "Getting back to the topic at hand — I like to see people together too, but, as I say, I share the man's viewpoint. I like to see them in crowds — at a football game, in a swimming pool, or just jostling each other on the subway. The more the much merrier, as we used to say." He looks to center stage again, perhaps this time out into the audience also. "I believe in the humankind — and in Life. Yeah, I believe in life — expressing itself everywhere at its best. — Melissa, you know what? — I think I'll become a — mankind server."*

THE WOMAN, *after more than half a minute. "Robbie."*

THE MAN, *his eyes still turned away, "What is it?"*

THE WOMAN, *"Let's talk."*

THE MAN, *still staring away, "Talk? O.K., let's talk. But what about?"*

THE WOMAN, *"About Life — Truth. About God!"*

THE MAN, *a nervous laugh and looking at her as though not believing his ears, "About — God? You're kidding!"*

THE WOMAN, *softly, carefully, "About us."*

THE MAN, *looking away, with impatience, "Are we to go through that again?"*

THE WOMAN, *her voice fraught with emotion, "It's — a girl's right — to expect such talk — we've been going together so long." The man's exasperation is apparent. "Oh, I know — we're not like other people, and I don't want to act like just another silly girl. But there comes a time when there has to be talk."*

THE MAN, *shifting impatiently in the booth, "What is there to talk about now? We've said everything."*

THE WOMAN, *studying his face and speaking carefully, "Everything, Robert?"*

THE MAN, *looking at her with slight anxiety now, "Everything. What else is there?"*

THE WOMAN, *"The most important thing. It has to be talked about sooner or later. Why not now?"*

THE MAN, *still apprehensive, yet his voice caught and quiet "O.K. — now — What is it?"*

THE WOMAN, *smiling and speaking softly, "Our being together — on a more permanent basis."*

THE MAN, *shifting in the booth as though to relieve tensions, "Go ahead — Why don't you say it?"*

THE WOMAN, *almost with small defiance, "O.K., I will. We have the right, the right to talk about it. It's not as though —"*

THE MAN, *evenly, coldly defiant, "Say it. Just go ahead and say it."*

THE WOMAN, *determined to have it out, "All right then — you and I married." As she says it she tries to look him evenly in the eyes. Her eyes waver and she* *looks away.*

THE MAN, *still speaking evenly, "You see. Even you know how wrong it would be. We're just not made for each other that way, Melissanda, not you and I — not permanently."*

THE WOMAN, *on the verge of nervous tears, "That's the silliest thing ever, Robert Douglas, and you know it. Who do you know that have been together longer and are better suited to each other? Why, we've been going together so long sometimes it seems we actually are —"*

THE MAN, *touched by a sense of guilt, "I tell you, Melissa, it would be no good. I'm married to my work. It will always be that way. After awhile you'd become miserable. It's just no good, Melissa."*

THE WOMAN, *tiny hysteria in her voice, "Good heavens! You talk as though something is wrong with you, with us. I'm not asking you to do something perverted. People get married every day, you know." She begins sobbing and puts her head down, ashamed. "There, you made me do it — you made me take the initiative."*

THE MAN, *unbelief and exasperation in his voice, "I made you take the initiative?"*

THE WOMAN, *through her crying, "Someone had to take it. You wouldn't."*

THE MAN, unbelief and wonder still in his voice, now enlarged, exaggerated, he speaks as though to the audience, "How do YOU like that? I made HER take the initiative?"

The woman sobs without control. Looking at her with edged eyes, gradually the man realizes the woman's crying is out of proportion to the situation, that something more than what has happened that afternoon is disturbing her. His hand hesitates at her hair. Troubled, a new sliver of fear in his voice, he speaks, "What is it, Melissa?" She raises her head a little as she goes on sobbing. He fondles her head uncertainly. "Tell me what it is. How can I help you if I don't know what it is?"

THE WOMAN, *"I didn't want it this way. I wanted you to ask me yourself because you wanted it." She breaks into sobbing again. The man's hand pauses in her hair. Watching her he says nothing. "What are we going to do, Robbie?"*

A sliver of fear has been pushing into the man's face as he begins to comprehend.

"I'm going to have a baby."

For a moment, even though his worst fear is confirmed, the man can't believe his ears. His face is distorted with his disbelief. And then, the thing unavoidable, he looks at her; he is immensely disturbed.

THE MAN, *"It's not true! It can't be true!"*

THE WOMAN, *sobbing, "True! True! True!" As though she were counting her miseries, "True!"*

They look at each other, drawn together with a sense of the hopelessness of their condition. The spotlight snaps off; gradually the stage lights up, revealing the present MAN and WOMAN at the coffee house table. The MAN is deeply moved, troubled, while the WOMAN looks on quietly, evenly.

THE MAN, choked up, "Was it really — like that?"

THE WOMAN, looking at HIM with a tender, even smile, "Yes — exactly — every word and every tear of it."

THE MAN, "I — I was a heel."

THE WOMAN, "No — just a normal young man who was desperately afraid to lose his freedom. After all, you already had from me all a girl can give the man she loves."

THE MAN, with great mortification, "Did I really say all those — boyish things?"

THE WOMAN, "About being married to YOUR work? Oh, yes, and meant them too. YOU see, I did let MYSELF think how silly YOU were to take what YOU read seriously. YOU actually lived some of those books... On a date, I had to guess, Was I with Martin Arrowsmith, Isaac Newton, or Pierre Curie. To make the evening a success, I had to playact Madame Curie." SHE laughs lightly.

"Just think, I might have become another Sara Bernhardt.

"Oh, yes, yes, YOU took yourself so seriously." With a tiny laugh, "YOU couldn't be content to be just another happy-go-lucky young man — YOU had to put your thumb in and change the universe.

"I had to put up with so much." A tiny laugh again. "As it turns out, the joke is on ME — DR. ROBERT DOUGLAS, the foremost nuclear physicist in America, perhaps in the world. In the whole world, ROBERT — just think, in the whole wide world." Laughing with light irony at herself.

All the while, the man shakes his head and says, "No — not true — if YOU only knew." But SHE goes on.

"You would have been — yes — such a catch, ROBERT, as WE used to say." Her voice catches again.

His face full of his emotions, the man reaches out to her urgently. The lights go down, and the spotlight is on center stage again: *The man and woman, a young man and young lady, standing side by side and holding hands. The man is very nervous and the woman is quiet, anxious, demure.*

She keeps looking hopefully into the man's face.

THE VOICE OVER THE P.A. SYSTEM AS THE JUSTICE OF THE PEACE, "Do you Robert Douglas, take this woman, Melissanda —"

VOICES OF THE MASQUERADERS AS A CHORUS:

Robbie's getting married!
Douglas is eloping!Robbie's going to marry! Robbie's going to marry!
Hi-ho, fiddle-yi-yo!
Melissanda's caught him and away they'll go!

THE MAN, *as the bridegroom, looking about on all sides with anxiety, "I* *wonder how they found out. And then followed us here."*

THE WOMAN, *looking to him, "Never mind them, Robbie — the justice of the peace now."*

THE VOICE OVER THE P.A. SYSTEM AS THE JUSTICE OF THE PEACE: attempting it again, his job, "Do you, Robert Douglas —"

VOICES OF THE MASQUERADERS AS A CHORUS:

Robbie's marrying Melissa!
Robbie and Melissa will be Douglas!
Robbie will be Mr. Douglas! Melissa will be Mrs. Douglas!

THE MAN, AS BRIDEGROOM, *real anxiety, almost anguish in his voice, "Those fools! What do they want of me?" The taunting voices continue.*

"You stay here. I'll be right back! I'll —I'll show them! I'll show them!" He speaks as though to both Melissanda and the Taunters.

He runs desperately, aimlessly toward the voices off stage. Sighing with apprehension, the woman looks after him. Finally, slowly, she turns her head in this direction and that, looking anxiously, desperately trying to see something. Her hand rises slowly to her mouth and she begins gnawing on it as she sobs quietly.

THE VOICE OVER THE LOUD SPEAKER AS JUSTICE OF THE PEACE: speaking slowly, gravely, yet also matter-of-factly, as though it were a common occurrence, "Looks like he's not coming back, doesn't it?"

THE WOMAN, *sobbing wildly now, looking about herself with desperate lostness, "Oh, no! No! No! No! No! No!"*

The spotlight snaps off and the floor lamp goes up. We see THE MAN and THE WOMAN. THE MAN is given over to feelings of guilt and mortification, while THE WOMAN sobs like HER younger self, that hopeless, given-up *No.* For a moment the light stays up and then, dimming down to darken out THE MAN, holds THE WOMAN's sobbing figure for seconds and goes out. Seconds later, the spotlight, the telephone, and THE WOMAN, as a glowing young lady at the peak of her youthfulness.

THE WOMAN, *speaking with a quiet vivacity, the telephone receiver held firmly and graciously in one hand at one ear!*

Oh, yes, Robert, Robert —
Yes, yes, — I say, yes —
A Church wedding? Darling, of course.
Yes, Yes — You better be there. (A happy lilt in her voice.)
Yes, yes — Just one moment till I —

VOICE OVER P.A. SYSTEM OF THE GOOD DOCTOR:

"Melissanda Mink! Miss Mink!"

As though wakened rudely from a sweet dream, THE WOMAN looks about and upwards, "Yes?"

VOICE OVER THE P.A. SYSTEM OF THE GOOD DOCTOR'

"You're at it again!"

THE WOMAN rises quietly, shamefacedly.

The spotlight snaps off and then stage lights go up. We see THE MAN and THE WOMAN on the settee. The man's look of mortification and guilt is changed to pity. THE WOMAN is sobbing, gusting with self-pity and desperation.

THE MAN, reaching to her, "Poor MELISSA! — If there were only a way of making it up to YOU!"

THE WOMAN, still sobbing, "Don't feel pity for ME! SHE attempts to move away from HIS gesture. "Don't feel pity for ME — for ME —" Her voice breaks.

THE MAN, as though repeating a talismanic chorus that would soothe all, "Poor, poor MELISSA."

THE WOMAN sobs for seconds more. And then, gradually, SHE raises HER head and sits up straight. As SHE does so, THE MAN's hand falls back slowly from HER. HE recovers gradually, yet it is evident the last scene has touched HIM deeply. HE lets his hand rest on HER arm now as though to prevent HER from sliding back into the anguish of the moments before.

THE WOMAN, trying to speak with composure but not succeeding, "But for moments at parties of mutual friends, that was the last time WE were really together. After YOU began to be successful in YOUR work, WE didn't see EACH OTHER again — up until today.

THE MAN, "I — I'm sorry, MELISSANDA. There is so much — blindness — and unintended cruelty in the world. WE never seem to know what WE really want — until — too late —"

THE WOMAN, in a tone of forgiveness and gracious understanding in HER voice now, "YOU cruel, ROBERT? Not at all. It was just that YOU had the courage to carry out what most bridegrooms feel. Unlike most, YOU didn't have to spend the rest of YOUR life being sorry."

THE MAN, looking at her evenly, "That's not true, MELISSANDA. MY life's been a torment ever since."

THE WOMAN, looking at HIM with a tiny smile, "Who, YOU, ROBERT DOUGLAS? — the golden boy of Barstowe and Cambridge, now foremost nuclear physicist in the East — in — a torment? Ha! That's a laugh, as WE used to say."

THE MAN, "It's true, MELISSANDA — a torment."

THE WOMAN, returning HIS even look, yet almost afraid of what SHE might see. HER voice carries a tiny note of hope, "Don't joke with ME, ROBERT."

THE MAN, almost afraid to speak, "The baby, MELISSANDA, what happened to the baby?"

THE WOMAN, coming out of the mood as though from a sleep, "What? Oh, the baby. There wasn't any. I guess I was mistaken, or —"

THE MAN, puzzled, "Wasn't any? But I thought —"

THE WOMAN, her voice quiet, tragic, "YOU see, ROBERT — I'd become so desperate about YOU, I tried to — trick YOU. If I couldn't have YOU any other way, there was always the last resort, the way of Eve."

THE MAN, not comprehending fully, "Trick ME?" And then his greatest compassion surging, "Oh, MELISSA — what — what fools the young and unknowing are!"

THE WOMAN, forcing a light laugh, "Yes, ROBERT. I, Melissanda Mink, the true-blue girl, finding that being guileless and sincere could not do it, decided to become like any other woman — to use the old stocks in trade." SHE begins sobbing again, this time hysterically.

THE MAN, with deep compassion, "MELISSA! MELISSA!" He makes a tender, protective movement to HER. SHE allows herself to be carried by the gesture.

Suddenly THE YOUNG WOMAN crosses the large windows inside.

THE WOMAN, "ROBERT, what time is it?"

THE MAN, "A few minutes after nine."

THE WOMAN, "That must be SHE," the door leading out to the terrace opening, "CHAR."

THE YOUNG WOMAN, standing on the top step of the stairway leading down to the terrace. SHE carries the glass of pink liquid. SHE's humming, "Cocktail time, Baby."

THE WOMAN, "CHAR, how do you always manage to do it? — Always, when YOU're needed most."

THE YOUNG WOMAN, "Wish a MAN would think that, just one MAN, any old MAN."

THE WOMAN, "But YOU sound so happy right now. How was YOUR report — to DOCTOR MALLOY? Or was it DOCTOR SANTENELLI this time? Groovy, I bet —"

THE YOUNG WOMAN, "Nah, DR. SANTELLI — you won't believe it but HE's an owl-eyed square — HIS name is wasted on HIM. Might as well have been DR. JONES or DR. MALLOY.

THE WOMAN, "But you seem so happy."

THE YOUNG WOMAN, "Happy? Yeah, I guess — A girl has to give herself consolation."

THE WOMAN, taking the medicine and sipping, "Poor CHAR." Then catching herself, "But don't give up, dear — Don't despair."

THE YOUNG WOMAN, "Who ME? — despair." To THE MAN, "Didja get a load of that, SHE suggesting that little ole animal ME could ever despair. Little ole dumb animal ME."

The curtain falls with THE WOMAN in an attitude of protector with THE YOUNG WOMAN, while THE MAN looks on with compassion.

THE END OF STAGE TWO

Stage III

The third week and THE MAN's third visit. THE MAN and THE WOMAN are seen coming into a coffee house specializing in coffees and teas of all nations. A WAITRESS takes them to a small, marble top table for two where they sit down. Around them, on all sides, hippies and yippies, reminiscent in attire and actions, in word and style of the masqueraders of STAGE I, but less extravagant and intense, but not much so. Characters who played the masqueraders play similar characters in the coffee house. As in the masquerades, couples act out fantasies, but here the fantasies seem realities. As for THE MAN and THE WOMAN, THEY seem to have been drawn closer by the past two visits and the intervening weeks. When THEY sit down, THEIR hands and knees touch spontaneously but quietly. The visit is no longer between old friends merely. Yet THE WOMAN still struggles to fend off the moment between THEM, while THE MAN seems to yield entirely. Turned to HER, HE watches THE WOMAN's face because it pleases HIM to do so.

THE WOMAN, "Last visit how we carried on about ME. You must forgive my self-involvement, ROBERT. It's one of the prices WE patients pay. Our needs are so taken care of WE become spoiled — WE forget others have needs too. YOU see, there I go again — I —"

THE MAN, "Not at all, Melissa. I came back today — to be with YOU, to hear about YOU. I've decided I need this more than anything else now."

THE WOMAN, looking for things in HIS face, "More than anything else what YOU need?"

THE MAN, "More than anything else. You see, MELISSA, success in the public sense often means failure in the private. Too often WE public servants never find out what our personal lives really need until it is almost too late."

THE WOMAN, laughing lightly, yet still watching his face, "Now who's being the clever one? Who's speaking in riddles?"

THE MAN, "I don't mean to be, believe ME, MELISSA. I want US to understand EACH OTHER without guess or doubt."

THE WOMAN, "Understand EACH OTHER?"

THE MAN, taking her hand, "Oh, MELISSA, it's not too late."

THE WOMAN, HER eyes searching his face, "YOU can't mean that, ROBERT. I guess YOU're the one who hasn't changed. OUR lives are almost at the point of running down. WE're at — that time of year, YOU know, ROBERT."

THE MAN, still speaking urgefully, "Oh, I know it's impossible to take up where WE left off — the clock can't be turned back. But — Oh, MELISSA, MELISSA, WE need EACH OTHER so much, YOU and I."

THE WOMAN, looking away quickly, "I'd like an expresso, please. Will YOU give my order, ROBERT?"
THE MAN, "Sure, sure. Waitress —"
THE WOMAN, as Robert gives an order for two expressos, "Tell ME, ROBERT, exactly what did happen that day? You know, in spite of time's healing hand and a woman's saving short memory for hurt, something inside her keeps wondering."
THE MAN, feeling guilt again, "I — an emotional coward, I guess. I wanted YOU so much, YOU know that — but there was always part of me that was afraid of something in OUR moments together. I was afraid of the overpowering unknown, I guess. Yet, yet, this has also been part of MY work — a wanting to find out about the unknown. The difference is in MY work I can weigh, test, and control from little to more and more — until, one day, if patience and application are great enough, I would have the very heart of THE ATOM at my fingertips."
THE WOMAN, a little sadly and wisely, "And you didn't think this was possible in our relationship."
THE MAN, "Oh, I know people make a happy go of marriage every day, and with much less — love than WE had. But it was because of OUR love that I was afraid. YOU see, MELISSA, it was as simple as this — I didn't think I had the right to experiment with or risk hurting YOUR life. If WE had become just another married couple — all excitement gone! — YOU having to wait eternally for a MAN who was away to HIS work, and, at night, lying at HIS side, not sleeping, wondering when it would end and YOUR life with him begin! — If this had happened, I don't think I could have lived with MYSELF. Our feelings were too important for ME to risk this. I think that was our trouble — WE loved each other too much."
THE WOMAN, with quiet wonder and pity, "You thought that?"
THE MAN, "No, I suppose I didn't think it all out that clearly. YOU see, MELISSANDA, all MY life I had known a WOMAN WHO gave me the same kind of love. Only with HER I could do nothing but go along in it — the burden, the sense of responsibility of living up to such love, such expectations! I didn't want to — I couldn't permit MYSELF to become involved permanently that way with another. Besides, I had nothing left to give, and YOUR life promised so much if I didn't interfere. It was the right time to decide, before it was too late."
THE WOMAN, "But don't YOU see — to be permitted to put HER life at the service of someone SHE loves is all the happiness a WOMAN wants. It is HER happiness. As much as a MAN and a WOMAN want and need EACH OTHER, they know they can't make that need their whole lives. A MAN and a WOMAN must find things to occupy the hours THEY're away from each other.

"Besides, it had already gone so far! To be deprived of the person you love, after your life has come to want and need and depend on HIM so much is much more agony than unhappiness or quiet desperation of the most hum-drum

marriage. At least SHE has HIM, if only for those brief moments at the table and in bed. At least they have each other, not for brief moments only, but for life."
THE MAN, "I know this now."
THE WOMAN, "I guess YOU were, in a way, younger than I. Poor MAN, how YOU must have suffered."
THE MAN, "If only I had, I would have been able to live with MYSELF better. I could have thought 'Serves you right — you had it coming!' But no, I was too single-minded to have felt punished, too intent on MY work to think or feel anything else. Oh, I guessed the truth about MYSELF — that I was trying to prove something by MY work, like — atoning for childhood guilt. But even knowing this I had to go on. Knowing an irritation of the chromosomes in the genes explains why I became a man rather than remaining an amoebe helps me to understand why I am what I am, but it does not change my need for acting as I do. It was only when my work had turned to ashes that I was really shaken. Even then I didn't allow MYSELF to think of the unhappiness I had caused you."
THE WOMAN, putting her hand on his with real compassion, "You poor, poor man — I'm so sorry for YOU — perhaps for both of US." Catching herself again, "But what about yourself — what have you been doing all this time?"
THE MAN, "About MYSELF?"
THE WOMAN, "What I haven't read in the newspapers."
THE MAN, "About MY work?"
THE WOMAN, "That, too, tell me about it."
THE MAN, regaining his composure slowly, "You wouldn't be —"
THE WOMAN, "Wouldn't be interested? Try ME and see. You know, Robert, shut away like this WE patients have no life on the outside to lay claim to. To make up for this, WE're at the radio, listening to the fiction of soap oepra, or at a newspaper, reading even the most insignificant human interest stories. A visitor presents an opportunity to reprieve ourselves. YOU see, after being shut away so long, WE lose our sense of things on the outside. WE welcome a visitor, with a double feeling — for the real excitement of his presence, and because a visit helps us to bring our ideas about the outside world — what it is like — back into line. You can't imagine what your visit means to a patient like myself —"
THE MAN, watches the woman with feeling as SHE speaks. Obviously continues to feel guilt, "MELISSA — I'm so —"
THE WOMAN, catching herself up, "So sorry? Don't be." Laughing lightly, "You mustn't be taken in by my emotionalism. You see — giving free wheel to OUR emotions now and then is another form of therapy. It's cathartic. It's like — passing water over carbon, to lure the gas out. Sometimes it gets out of hand —"
THE MAN, "MELISSANDA — I —"
THE WOMAN, "But look, now, WE're right back to ME. Isn't it curious how, no matter where WE start off, our talk always manages to come back to ME. It's

as though in my state of nerves and emotions I've become society's thing to be argued. I've become the measure of all things sad.'' SHE laughs with a tone of self-pity and small tragedy.

THE MAN, "It's all right, MELISSANDA — I — understand. If only —"

THE WOMAN, breaks in as though afraid of what he was about to say. "But WE mustn't let it be that way, must WE? —not good for either of US, or for the outside world — especially not for the world inside, the world of rooms." SHE takes a determined hold on HER emotions.

THE MAN, a little embarrassed, "MELISSANDA — "

THE WOMAN, "No, I've had my little emotional cathartic. You mustn't encourage ME. YOU must help ME to get outside MYSELF, at least for now — Please, ROBERT —

THE MAN, making a great effort, "Somehow it seems like a schoolboy recitation — out of one of those brightly colored, new-smelling linen books WE used to read, *THE LIVES OF FAMOUS MEN,* printed in large caps on glossy paper."

THE WOMAN, tutting lightly as SHE prepares HERSELF to listen. However, HER eyes betray an inward turning mind. It's a look often seen in the blind. "Now, now — ROBERT — remember, I'm the patient, not YOU." The latter with a small, tragic smile.

THE MAN, "Yes, YOU're the patient — not I. YOU the patient, not —"

THE WOMAN, her smile becoming more and more reflective as the man goes on, "I, the patient, not YOU." The exchange like a schoolroom prompting — MELISSANDA, the teacher, and ROBERT, the pupil.

THE MAN, clearing his throat, "Very well." (In the voice of a schoolboy reciting his lesson for the day, *"At school I took all honors. Whatever stipends were available to young research scientists in nuclear physics were available to me. My research heads called me first name, Robert, and I, after a while, found myself calling them first name, Robert, Henry, or Bill. For five years this was my entire life. And, of course, always my research, my special project. I found after the first year that I did my best work, had the greatest quota of personal concentration after seven o'clock in the evening — from seven in the evening to two in the morning, to be exact. And so, along with a handful of others, I undertook a night time regimen that stayed with me the rest of my life."*

As HE talks, we have the sense of THE WOMAN listening less and less. HER eyes become distant. Every now and again, the stage lights go down, and the spotlight holds center stage, giving us another scene from THE WOMAN's past. THE MAN continues his monologue during each of the following scenes, just as if nothing else were happening. Yet, HE reacts to the center stage scenes with a growing intensity. HIS recitation is no longer in the voice of a schoolboy. HE looks into the woman's face with greater emotions and reaches out to HER more and more.

Stage lights go down as the man recites. Lights center stage go up, and we see THE WOMAN, alone. SHE is quite entirely alone. There is no dialogue in this scene, no sound at all — just the man reciting and THE WOMAN alone. This is the action, this is the dialogue, this is the drama of the scene, THE WOMAN walking about, alone. The center stage light holds HER for a minute or so and then snaps off. Stage lights go up again, revealing THE WOMAN and THE MAN.

THE MAN, watching her, yet going on with the recitation, *"Princeton — OPPENHEIMER and the old boy himself, ALBERT EINSTEIN, something of a little god for me, until I met him on the occasional few times HE appeared and disappeared through our laboratories. Actually HE looked more like a vague featured grandmother or a friendly, abstract-eyed miniature St. Bernard, also* a deus ex machina — *Yet, HE was always a noble reminder from the past of what I was up to. The Research Foundation — THEY told me I had carte blanche, all facilities at my service and a perpetual congregation of the great and the near great in MY own and related fields as MY confreres and advisors. WE were special, a knightly order upon whom society turned its hopeful eyes. OUR mission was special, almost portentious. As the direction of OUR work became clearer, there were times when WE actually felt the most important things about life were being determined not in the offices of ambassadors and statesmen, not in Washington, London, or Berlin, but at the tips of OUR fingers, on the fringes of OUR minds.*

Stage lights dim, followed by the spotlighting of center stage, front. We see **THE WOMAN, drink in hand, sitting on an ottoman. SHE exudes an air of alcoholic party mood, a little too primed, perhaps, a little desperate. Before HER, a SUAVE MAN, a typical party hound who commands all the surface kindnesses and attentions that a YOUNG WOMAN finds increasingly appealing as SHE gets on in HER mid twenties of bachelor WOMANHOOD.**

THE WOMAN, her face softly attentive and interested, "Oh, yes, yes — that would be so nice — A trip together, as you say, JOCKO, to France." SHE takes a quick drag on her cigarette, "And then to Italy. There WE shall —"

THE MAN, fixing her with softly smiling eyes, "In France, we shall first of all see Paris — the Eiffel Tower, the Boulevard Montparnasse —"

THE WOMAN, eagerly, almost girlishly, "Yes, yes — the Eiffel Tower and the Boulevard Montparnasse —"

THE MAN, "The *Deux Magots* and all of Left Bank sinning." with a suggestive look.

THE WOMAN, "Yes, yes — and then where?"

THE MAN, weaving his spell, "Then — since we have done all this — then to the wooden shoe paysage of Bretagne — a *pension,* where we

can *vivre ensemble.*"
THE WOMAN, reciting in an excited little girl's voice, "Oh, yes" and she recites —

"Mon enfant, ma soeur,
Songe à la douceur —"

THE MAN:

"D'aller la-bas
Vivre ensemble."

THE WOMAN, rushing to the end, her voice quiet yet excited,

"La, toute n'est qu'ordre et beauté —"

THE MAN, taking her softly by the arm:

"Luxe, calme, et volupté."

"Shall we go for a walk in the garden?"
THE WOMAN, permitting herself to be raised to her feet, she falls in submissively at his side as he puts his arms about her and recites quietly, "*Luxe, calme, et volupté.* It sounds — so easy in French." The bright center stage light dims as THEY go walking langorously across left stage, round and about, more and more slowly. The stage is blacked out. Seconds later, the bright center stage light goes up. *Again the telephone is prominent, with the woman, looking in the first flush of womanhood, radiant, softly contained yet excited as she takes the receiver from the saddle. SHE holds the receiver as though SHE and the telephone knew something together, about each other.*
THE WOMAN, a YOUNG WIFE and NEWLY-MADE-MOTHER voice:

Yes, ROBERT, darling, yes — A girl;
I'm sorry YOUR work kept YOU
From being here — But it was alright, yes;
I could, darling, sense YOU so near —
It's a girl, darling, yes — seven pounds —
Now I can put away this belly-ful dress.

The light snaps out. Seconds later, the stage lights go up. Turned full face to THE WOMAN, THE MAN still recites, but now a little apologetically, haltingly, as though forced to continue an affront. Something in THE WOMAN's face tells HIM HE must go on.

THE MAN, "Those first years in the Institute were so difficult. Everything learned in graduate school had to be unlearned, new ways learned in their place. The only thing that remained constant was the awareness that what WE were after was both specific and concrete and also vague and mysterious.

"The real beginning came when I presented MY paper on the findings of the first three years of MY project before the Institute as a whole, a convocation, an exchange of findings.

The stage lights go down and the bright spot holds center stage. We discover

THE WOMAN in the arms of a MAN. THEY are dancing, slowly, intimately, to a langorous fox trot that carries the air of things always beginning and ending in the moment. THE MAN is a paragon of smoothness. Exuding a sense of good whiskey and freshly barbered hair and pomade, HE seems to know what HE is doing every moment. THEY talk in hushed, intimate voices. As THEY talk, THEY dance more and more slowly until, fully enclosed in each other's arms, THEY sway with a soft rhythm in a single spot. THE WOMAN's attitude is that of yielding responsiveness, while THE MAN's is that of an easy possessor. He's obviously used to possessing, to being said *yes* to.

THE MAN, hums softly in her ear, then speaks, "Come here often?"
THE WOMAN, "Whenever things get a little too routine —"
THE MAN, "Uh — huhn. Who are you?"
THE WOMAN, "You mean my name, or what I do?"
THE MAN, "Name — What you do — Both."
THE WOMAN, Melissanda. I'm a teacher. But don't hold that against me."
THE MAN, "Oh, I see." And then with a soft after-thought. "But teachers are human too."
THE WOMAN, "Yes, human too. We like our time away from it all."
THE MAN, "You came to the right place for it. It's the lights, so low, and the music, so real soft and inviting —"
THE WOMAN, "Yes, so very real soft — and inviting. Your name? No, don't tell me — better that way."
THE MAN, "The feel of it: just you, the music, and the person you're with — you and me — You can call me Gerald."
THE WOMAN, "Yes, just the music and — Gerald — that's a nice name."
THE MAN, "My car is outside. Could go to my place. Have a choice record collection and a bottle of the best Chives Regal. A mellow drink, soft music, and just you and me together, dancing — and —"

They dance more and more slowly round and about, each turn carrying them closer to the off-stage door. The spotlight snaps down, dropping the stage into soft, insinuating shadows, then into blackness.

When the spotlight goes up again, the scene is center stage at the telephone. We see THE WOMAN, *matronly now, a woman who has done her fullest duty as a wife and mother. She lifts the receiver as though it were a familiar and secure friend.*

THE WOMAN;

So pleased, Robert, yes —
So wonderfully, wonderfully pleased.
A boy, Robert, yes — your eyes,
Oh, yes — most certainly your eyes,
Oh, yes — And yes, certainly,

To call him Robbie. And now once more
To put away this special duty dress.

The spotlight goes down, slowly, lingeringly. Once again we have the terrace scene. We see THE MAN and THE WOMAN. THE WOMAN looks bemused, a little tragic, THE MAN is given to HIS emotions.

THE MAN, "MELISSANDA, listen to ME —"

THE WOMAN, absently, "Yes, ROBERT, I'm listening." As though contemplating something distant.

THE MAN, with desperation, "Oh, God! What can I say?"

THE WOMAN, "As YOU were saying, Robert, about YOUR work —"

THE MAN, looks at her searchingly. Finally HE goes on, reluctantly, as though forced to perform a sacrilege, **"The Manhattan Project. They told ME I was one of the half dozen *brilliant young physicists* who had been selected after being watched over the years. The Manhattan Project. I don't think anyone can fully imagine the sense of overwhelming responsibility and awe WE experienced when we guessed the nature of our assignment. The war going on all around us outside, WE were led to feel it was our contribution to the war effort. More than that, WE were impressed with the fact that the very existence of life as WE knew it depended upon it. WE said, yes, just as though WE actually had a choice. WE went along — to — perform our duty. Also, the Project was in the direct line of OUR research of the past ten or fifteen years. WE had no choice — WE had to follow objective research wherever it led US."**

THE WOMAN, her smile bemused and knowing, "Yes, to follow it wherever it led US —"

THE MAN, "Few of US anticipated what happened later —"

THE WOMAN, a look of tiny tragedy in her face, "No, not at all to anticipate what happened later —"

The lights go down. Again, the spotlight center stage, and the woman, thirtyish, already beginning to look like the efficient school teacher she had become. Her competence shows through even during the hours of relaxation, even during the evening, to which the daylight hours are only a prologue. She sits on a couch in a living room. Next to her is a man. Also thirtyish, he is not efficient looking, nor does he seem competent, not even in his manhood. Somewhat small, he is not quite taller than the woman. He is uncertain of himself. His urges of expression easily become urges to withdraw. Depending upon his needs of the moment, the woman's responses are alternately those of a little girl and those of a mother.

THE WOMAN, in a full, mother-tutting voice, yet patient and tolerant, "But we hardly know each other, Jack."

THE MAN, trying to look at her with conviction and great sincerity, "A man knows — almost from the first moment. He looks and looks — finally one day he sees her and he — knows."

THE WOMAN, touched, "But you hardly know what I'm like. How do you know I'm right for you?"

THE MAN, "I want you so much, Melissanda. I need you so much, Melissanda." His gesture to her is incomplete. It is as much of an advance as he can make without being encouraged and guided by a large response from the woman.

THE WOMAN, speaking softly and a little coyly now, "But it's sort of like — putting the cart before the horse, isn't it?"

THE MAN, urgefully, moving closer to her, "Oh, Melissanda — I want you so. We could be happy together — we could be so happy together."

THE WOMAN, in a little girl's voice, melting and coy, both, "Who? You and little old school teacherish me? Happy together?"

THE MAN, embracing her awkwardly, "Oh, Melissanda! Melissanda! My woman! My — wife!"

They embrace, fumblingly, awkwardly. The woman has to lead him until his passion takes over. The light goes down slowly, then snaps off. A minute or so later, the light goes up and we have *the scene at the telephone: the woman, matronly, at her ripest.*

THE WOMAN, *less triumph than the last telephone scene is apparent, yet she shows satisfaction.*

And now, Robert, yes again — six pounds —
This time again safely done.
What, Robert? No, a girl — a girl, Robert, yes —
Another girl, Robert, yes —
After this, I'll need a new mother dress.

The light at the telephone goes off. Gradually we're back on the terrace as the stage lights go up. THE MAN talks without verve. HIS emotions are too great for HIM to go on, but again something in THE WOMAN's face, half listening, half musing, makes him continue. As HE speaks, HE looks to center stage with apprehension. HE is also apprehensive of what HE might see in THE WOMAN's face.

THE MAN, "The Manhattan Project — the FISSION of THE ATOM — the breaking open of the very heart of energy and life itself. Few of US had expected IT would be put to destructive use. Few expected Hiroshima, Nagasacki. Few of US, only the most dehumanized, those most cut-off from the outside world, expected the solution of life's greatest secret, how energy is held together, would be put to such life-destroying use —"

The lights go down and the spotlight, center stage, goes up, holding the woman again, now sitting with a man in an officer's uniform, any branch of the armed service. They might be in the back seat of a car. She is in her early thirties. Her femininity seems to be stimulated artificially by alcohol and such. Her dress and make-up show extra care. The man has also been drinking heavily. He is big and confident of the urges he experiences with the woman. He embraces her passionately while she yields to him readily, letting herself be carried by his urges.

THE WOMAN, her speech is thick and heavy with alcohol and passion, "You're so — much a man. So — big."

THE MAN, with a sense of the power he holds over the woman, "And you're so much a woman, a real, giving woman. It's never been so good before — never, never so good before." Her arms about him tightly, the woman gives more and more of herself. As the man keeps taking her, he murmurs, "Never before so good." The light dims and then comes up again. *THE WOMAN is at the telephone.*

THE WOMAN, *with a sense of the fullest satisfaction, as though there could be no greater fulfillment of HER WOMANHOOD.*

Oh, Robert, yes — most certainly —
Now again — a boy — a boy, Robert, a boy —
Yes, a boy — so big I almost split my dress.

The spotlight goes down and then up again. We see the woman and a man. Big like the former, but not in uniform, he is more insistent about his passion. He takes everything into forceful control; the woman is overwhelmed. The few words they speak are thick and slurred. They embrace almost roughly.

THE WOMAN, "Oh, darling, darling."

THE MAN, "Oh, God! Where have you been all my life?"

THE WOMAN, "If only all men were like you. If only — Darling, oh, darling — you feel so good!"

The light goes down, then up. We see *THE WOMAN at the telephone.*

THE WOMAN, *a sense of filling her fullest role as a WOMAN,*

Another Robert — yes, another —
Another boy, Robert,yes — another —
One more, yes.

The spotlight goes off. The stage light goes up, showing THE MAN and THE WOMAN of present time. THE MAN seems unable to go on. THE WOMAN smiles with slight pathos. SHE is still only half listening.

THE WOMAN, HER face half turned to him, "Yes, ROBERT — go on — as you were saying."

THE MAN, his emotions overwhelming his efforts at speech, "Melissanda — I — I —"

THE WOMAN, "Yes, ROBERT, as YOU were saying — THE ATOM BOMB."

THE MAN, finally getting control of HIMSELF. HE looks apprehensively from THE WOMAN's face to center stage and then back to HER face again, **"THE ATOM BOMB — but even then some of US still hoped. OUR thoughts**

were an evasion of what WE knew was certain to develop. With dream thinking," HE glances to center stage, "WE tried to rationalize away OUR guilt and responsibility.

"The former GREAT HOPES of our society, the PATHFINDERS in the FRONTIERS of NUCLEAR PHYSICS, WE did our work mostly because WE had to but also with the silent hope that sanity would prevail and good would result. Yet always WE silently feared the worst. The worst did happen: WE began doing things with FUSION. WE knew then it was hopeless: the slide had begun and would not end until it was done. With THE HYDROGEN BOMB, for the first time the destruction of civilization became possible —"

Stage lights dim as the scene center stage emerges in the spotlight. The spotlight is overbright, unreal, as though burning with a hyperintense fever. We see the woman and a man, continuingly embracing. The only words, the woman's, are coarse and drunken.

THE WOMAN, "More, darling boy — more."
THE MAN, embracing her roughly, "Mmmmm!"
THE WOMAN, "More! More!"

The light goes down, then up, giving us the scene at the telephone.

THE WOMAN, *"A boy — Robert, dear, yes, another boy —"*

The light goes down, then up again, and again the woman with another man. The two embracing, this time the woman takes the initiative. Her embraces are avid, famished. During the split seconds of the scene, all we hear is her coarsened, drunken voice, **"Oh, God! More!".**

Again the light goes down, then up, giving us the telephone scene, THE WOMAN saying into the phone, *"A boy again, Robert — how wonderful, a boy again!"*

A MAN's voice comes from the P.A. system, calling to THE WOMAN. THE WOMAN does not seem to hear as the above two scenes are repeated. A MAN's voice on the P.A. system grows louder and more insistent. Still THE WOMAN does not hear. In the midst of the second telephone scene, the voice of a man from the stage audience circling at the back, "Oh, God! I can't take any more! The freaks!" A yippie breaks away from the stage audience and runs off stage. The spotlight snaps off; stage lights go up. Sobbing THE MAN sits with his head in his hands. THE WOMAN looks at him with wonder and pity as HE says, "I've killed Life! I've killed Life!" Shattered, HIS voice breaks up with sobs.

THE WOMAN, "Poor ROBERT! It's disturbed YOU —I'm sorry. I should have known as an outsider YOU wouldn't be able to take many of them. Being used to them and feeling the cleansing we sometimes forget it isn't quite the same for outsiders. I am sorry."

THE MAN, with anguish, "Oh, God! I've destroyed our one chance for salvation, MELISSANDA — I had it right here in MY hand and what did I do? I made a — monster of it. (Sobs.) Then looking up — a hurt plea in his voice. Let's undo it all TOGETHER, MELISSANDA. It's not too late."

SHE gestures about the coffee house to the hippies and yippies. "Is anything so

THE WOMAN, caressing his bowed head, "Poor Robert! Experiencing middle-aged guilt and loneliness, as the GOOD DOCTOR might put it. You had everything to begin with and I had nothing. All I ever wanted was to make the most of MY little nothing, while you always wanted more. And now I've made MY peace with my nothing, while YOU still want more."

THE MAN, overwrought sincerity, "Let's make up for everything, Melissanda — we can get married.

THE WOMAN, laughing lightly, the humor directed at herself, "Marry, Robert? And at OUR age?. . . I don't think I really need it now —" After a pause. "Remember how YOU used to put it sometimes? Pooh-poohing the idea of love, YOU said it was merely the chemistry of the thing that did it. The chemistry, remember, Robert, the physics of the thing. Sometimes when YOU looked at me, I felt like so much blood corpuscles, nervous responses and body chemistry. It's not very flattering to a girl — it takes away HER incentive. . . And now that's all changed, isn't it? — No more chemistry now." Her voice catches. "I'm quite free of the whole thing now. And with this freedom I've freed myself of YOU, ROBERT. Free — free — you hear? But it wasn't only YOU, ROBERT. YOU were not my neurosis — you were merely a symptom of it. As I now am of YOUR present neurosis. You know, Robert, that's not really a sign of — soundness — to come to a looney house in search of a BRIDE."

THE MAN, his face working with strong emotions, "That's just it — this place. Let ME take YOU away."

THE WOMAN, "Take me away from the nursing home right now? For what?" She gestures about the coffee house to the hippies and yippies. "Is anything so very much different here than it is in the home nowadays? In the home, at least, I have all my needs taken care of — my little room with my T-V set, books and records, three meals a day, DOCTORS to pay me nice little visits, and when I want more company I can go to one of the public rooms and join in the fun or go out on the grounds for a walk, alone or with CHAR." Suddenly, as with an afterthought. "The time, ROBERT? What time is it?"

THE MAN, "A few minutes before —"

THE WOMAN, "So late? And so quick? Will you — take me back, ROBERT?"

THE MAN, "Take you back?" He looks at her quickly, hopefully.

THE WOMAN, "To the nursing home. It's time to take my medicine. My medicine, ROBERT."

THE MAN, with emotion, "Yes, yes, I'll take you back, MELISSA. MELISSA, I'll take YOU back." They stand together side by side, absolutely still for seconds.

THE MAN, finally says it, "What did it to YOU, MELISSA? Was it me? Was I the trouble?"

THE WOMAN, a moment, and then, turning away from him, "It was not just you, ROBERT — It was — everything — nothing — Still is. But now that I know what it is, I can wait until I am free of it too — just as I have freed myself of YOU. And now that I have, everything seems just so — at least for now — MY condition, the nursing home, and even the sounds of the building going up next to it — new things, new hope! And that's as it should be. As for tomorrow — well, let's see what tomorrow brings."

As she talks they leave the coffee house and cross the way to the nursing home. They are met on the steps by the YOUNG WOMAN.

THE WOMAN, at the sight of the YOUNG WOMAN, "Oh, CHAR — are WE late again?" CHAR — won't you forgive me?" She smiles warmly as though to a big sister, or even a daughter, as she takes the glass from the YOUNG WOMAN. Sipping, the woman turns to THE MAN.

THE WOMAN, putting her glass down without finishing it, "Leaving, ROBERT? I guess it is almost time." She looks questioningly to the YOUNG WOMAN.

THE YOUNG WOMAN, "You have a few minutes more. Still on curfew — still another month of curfew for YOU."

THE WOMAN, "Yes, still on curfew." Then to THE MAN, "You see, they look after us well —"

THE MAN, "MELISSANDA — I — Take care of yourself. It's been so good seeing YOU after all these years. YOU — YOU've scarcely changed, still the MELISSANDA WE all knew and loved.

THE WOMAN, laughing girlishly, "Thank you, ROBERT. I feel so good now I'll permit myself the luxury of enjoying the flattery. YOU always did know what to say to please a girl —"

THE MAN, moving toward the door, "Good-by, MELISSANDA. Take care of YOURSELF — And — I — I — "

THE WOMAN, her voice warm, poised, "Good-by, ROBERT — Do come for another visit soon. It helped so much, does so much for us, you know. It's been so much help — seeing YOU again." HER voice catches. ROBERT at the door, her hand comes to her mouth. "Robert!" He stops with his hand on the doorknob.

THE MAN, hopefully, "Yes, MELISSA."

THE WOMAN, her voice overcharged with emotion, "Don't tell GOD where I am!" Her voice dips and then breaks.

THE MAN, terror in his voice, "God? Who's God?"

THE MAN goes out the door and pulls it closed, slowly and quietly. Momentarily the woman looks at the closed door, perhaps a little wistfully. She listens to the departing clack of his heels, blending with the sounds of the pneumatic drill.

THE WOMAN, voice still shaky — gets a hold of herself gradually, "There goes a real fine specimen of a man — one of the world's foremost authorities on nuclear physics. It was so good to see HIM again after all these years." She sighs deeply and sips at her glass. A thought coming to her, she puts the glass down and turns to the nurse, brightly.

"In the excitement, I almost forgot — How is it now with YOU and DR. WASHINGTON? Or is it DR. RABINOWITZ or DR. RODRIGUEZ this time?"

She speaks as though she has seen good news in the young woman's face.

THE YOUNG WOMAN, laughing with quick delight, "DR. WASHINGTON — HE really surprised ME, that midnight flyer." The lilt, soft, self-assured in HER body, "HE asked me to go to the Sunday concert with him. Imagine, little, ole dumb-animal ME!"

THE WOMAN, a full smile, with warmth, "There, there, you see — There was nothing to worry about. Sometimes it isn't just one thing they want us for. Sometimes they do see us for what we really are. You see, everything does come out all right in the end, doesn't it? The new building, CHAR — Have you noticed it? It's almost completed.

THE YOUNG WOMAN, self-involved, "Imagine, little ole dumb-animal ME — little ole dumb animal ME! — A nurse catching a PSYCHIATRIST! Imagine!"

A pause here as the action comes to a closing.